# Explore

CCSS/PARCC Prep
# Grade 5 Reading

by Dr. James E. Swalm and Dr. June I. Coultas

with Patricia Braccio and Kathleen Haughey

Edited by Rick Kantrowitz and Sarah M.W. Espano

Designed by Nancy C. Goroff

Queue, Inc • 80 Hathaway Drive • Stratford CT 06615
Phone 800 232 2224 • Fax 800 775 2729

www.qworkbooks.com

## THE AUTHORS

**Dr. James Swalm** has been actively involved in the development of classroom instructional materials for many years. As Director of the New Jersey Right to Read and Bureau of Basic Skills, he participated in the development of statewide tests in reading, writing and mathematics as well as in the writing of various instructional and staff development materials in reading and language arts. Dr. Swalm has authored and co-authored numerous books and professional articles on reading, writing, and assessment, as well as on the use of technology in instruction. He has taught both undergraduate and graduate level courses in reading and curriculum development, and at all levels, K–12. Dr. Swalm has also been a principal, assistant superintendent, and superintendent, and has served as an educational consultant to many school districts.

**Dr. June I. Coultas** is well-known in the field of education and curriculum development. Her many positions include that of teacher, director of curriculum and instruction, college professor, consultant, lecturer, and award-winning grant writer. She is the author and co-author of numerous educational books, as well as of multimedia software programs. Her career includes being New Jersey director of the federal Right-to-Read Program, and manager of the state Bureau of Basic Skills. In addition to memberships in numerous professional associations, she is a past president of the New Jersey Reading Association.

Acknowledgments
Illustrations
Carl W. Swanson, Ph.D.
Maureen B. Coultas
Sarah J. Holden

Poems
Glenn G. Coats, M. Ed.
Jonathan D. Kantrowitz

Class Pack ISBN: 978-0-7827-2341-0 • Student Book ISBN: 978-0-7827-2340-3 • Copyright © 2014 Queue, Inc.
Whiteboard/Workbook Class Pack ISBN: 978-0-7827-2547-6 • Standalone Whiteboard ISBN: 978-0-7827-2546-9

# Table of Contents

# Table of Contents

# Test-Taking Tips

**Tips for Answering Multiple-Choice Questions**
Multiple-choice questions have a **stem,** which is a question or an incomplete sentence, followed by four answer choices. You should select only one answer choice. Here are some tips to help you correctly answer multiple-choice questions on the Common Core English Language Arts Test:

- Read each passage carefully.
- Read each question and think about the answer. You may look back to the reading selection as often as necessary.
- Answer all questions on your answer sheet. Do not mark any answers to questions in your test booklet.
- For each question, choose the best answer, and completely fill in the circle in the space provided on your answer sheet.
- If you do not know the answer to a question, skip it and go on. You may return to it later if you have time.
- If you finish the section of the test that you are working on early, you may review your answers in that section only. Don't go on to the next section.

**Checklist for Answering Open-Ended Questions**
- Keep the central idea or topic in mind.
- Keep your audience in mind.
- Support your ideas with details, explanations, and examples.
- State your ideas in a clear sequence.
- Include an opening and a closing.
- Use a variety of words and vary your sentence structure.
- State your opinion or conclusion clearly.
- Capitalize, spell, and use punctuation correctly.
- Write neatly.

# CHAPTER 1

# Text Elements
## Theme, Central Idea, and Supporting Details

**RL.5.1; RI.5.1: RECOGNITION OF SUPPORTING DETAILS**
**RL.5.2; RI.5.2: RECOGNITION OF THEME OR CENTRAL IDEA**

Reading is a skill that you are well on your way to mastering. When reading a passage, you should know how to identify the **theme**, **central idea**, and **supporting details**.

Every passage you will read in this workbook will have a central idea or theme. Many of the questions you will be asked will have to do with identifying the central idea or theme.

## YOU TRY IT

You have just finished reading a story in class. Your teacher asks you to write a sentence or paragraph stating the central idea of the story. How do you answer?

- Do you tell everything that happened in the story?
- Do you identify the important characters?
- Do you write about why the story was written and what message it is communicating?

Your best strategy would be to think about what the moral, lesson, or big idea was in the story. In other words, follow the third suggestion and write about why the story was written and what message it is communicating.

---

## RL.5.2; RI.5.2: RECOGNITION OF THEME OR CENTRAL IDEA

### What is a theme or central idea?

A **theme**, or **central idea**, can be thought of as the "big idea" in a reading passage. It is what that particular passage is mainly about.

Sometimes the theme, or central idea, is stated in the passage. Other times the theme, or central idea, is not stated and the reader has to infer it. Throughout the text there are clues that help the reader understand the theme, or central idea.

**Examples of a theme, or central idea, statement include:**
- One good deed leads to another.
- Treat others the way you would like to be treated.
- Animals can adapt to their environment in unusual ways.

**Here are some ways to find the theme, or central idea:**
- Look at the title of the passage or the story. Sometimes this will give you clues about the theme, or central idea.
- Notice the details in the passage or the story. What greater meaning might they be pointing to? This larger meaning is often the central idea or theme.
- Try to write a headline, or a sentence, of less than five words to explain what the passage is about.

**Explore CCSS/PARCC Grade 5 Reading** © 2014 Queue, Inc. All rights reserved.

# RL.5.1; RI.5.1: RECOGNITION OF SUPPORTING DETAILS

## What are supporting details?

**Supporting details** are ideas or information that build upon or explain the central idea.

To get a message across, an author uses details to explain his or her point of view.

These details could be facts or additional parts of the story that build upon the central idea.

It is usually best to find the central idea first; that will make it easier to determine which sentences include the supporting details.

**The paragraph below is an example to show supporting details:**

> Today, Tampa International Airport is one of the busiest airports in the country. Thousands of travelers pass through its halls and stations every day. Many giant jet airplanes and skilled pilots fly from the airport to cities all over the world. This is quite a change from the airport as it once was. When the airport began in 1914, it had only one pilot, Tony Jannus, and one small plane.

The central idea of this paragraph is that the airport in Tampa, Florida, has dramatically changed over the years.

**The supporting details are:**
• When the airport began in 1914, it had only one pilot and one small plane.
• Thousands of travelers pass through its busy halls and stations every day.
• Today, many giant jet airplanes and skilled pilots fly from the airport to cities all over the world.

## LET'S TRY IT TOGETHER

> **DIRECTIONS**   Read the story/passage and together we will discuss the questions.

# The Stag at the Pool *from Aesop's Fables*

A stag overpowered by heat came to a spring to drink. Seeing his own shadow reflected in the water, he greatly admired the size and variety of his antlers, but felt angry with himself for having such slender and weak feet.

While he was thus contemplating himself, a lion appeared at the pool and crouched to spring upon him. The Stag immediately took to flight, and exerting his utmost speed, as long as the plain was smooth and open, kept himself easily at a safe distance from the Lion.

But entering the woods, he became entangled by his horns, and the Lion quickly came up to him and caught him. When too late, he thus reproached himself: "Woe is me! How I have deceived myself! These feet which would have saved me I despised, and I gloried in these antlers which have proved my destruction." ∎

**Explore CCSS/PARCC Grade 5 Reading** © 2014 Queue, Inc. All rights reserved.

## What is the central idea of this story?

**Is it that the Stag was thirsty and came to drink?**
No, that is not the central idea. Although it is the way the story begins, it does not tell us what the story is about.

**Is it that a lion interrupted the Stag?**
The fact that the Lion interrupted the Stag while he was drinking is a supporting detail. It is not the central idea.

**Is it that the Lion chased the Stag into a wood?**
The fact that the Lion chased the Stag across the plain and into a wood is a supporting detail, not the theme, or central idea.

**Is it that the Stag should have accepted himself for who he was?**
Yes! That is the theme, or central idea of the story. While looking in the water, the Stag critiqued his figure, admiring his horns and criticizing his legs. He was so distracted that he did not notice that danger was near.

It was the part of his body he thought the least of—his legs—that proved to be his best asset in getting away from the Lion. The story is reminding readers to accept themselves for who or what they are. Sometimes it could be the thing you like least about yourself that is your best quality.

If you look at the entire story, you will notice that all of the details go back to and support this idea.

## What are the supporting details?

Let's use a graphic organizer to sort out the supporting details from this story.

The Stag admires his antlers and criticizes his legs and feet.

▼

The Lion comes upon the Stag.

▼

The Stag outruns the Lion on the plain.

▼

The Lion is looking for a way to trap the Stag.

▼

The Stag enters a wood and his antlers get caught.

## YOU TRY IT

> **DIRECTIONS**  Read the passage below and answer the questions that follow.

# Sir Francis Chichester

Francis Chichester was born in Dover, which is on England's coast. Therefore, it wasn't unusual that he would have developed an interest in sailing. It would be many years before Francis would gain fame as a sailor, not until he was 59 years old. And his most famous adventure took place when he was 65.

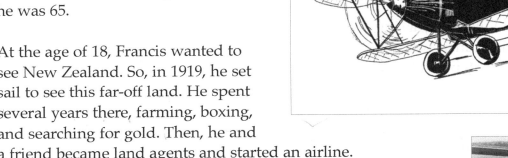

At the age of 18, Francis wanted to see New Zealand. So, in 1919, he set sail to see this far-off land. He spent several years there, farming, boxing, and searching for gold. Then, he and a friend became land agents and started an airline.

*Gipsy Moth*

In 1929, Francis returned to England. It was there that he began to pursue his dream—to fly. Three months after getting his license, Francis flew a biplane by himself from England to Sydney, Australia. Next, he made the first solo flight from New Zealand to Australia. His small single engine plane was named *Gipsy Moth*.

*Francis Chichester with his seaplane, the* **Gipsy Moth**

Francis had even bigger plans. He wanted to fly alone around the world. At the time, flying was still very new. Therefore, there were only a few places to land airplanes along the way. Francis knew that the only way to make the trip was in a seaplane. So, he added pontoons to the *Gipsy Moth*. Pontoons are floats fitted to an aircraft to allow it to land on water.

> ✔ **CHECK FOR UNDERSTANDING**
>
> Why do you think Francis thought that the best way to travel the world would be by plane?

Francis learned to fly the seaplane. He took off from

---

Australia. He was the first to travel to Japan by himself. However, his round-the-world flight ended there. After hitting telegraph wires, his plane crashed into Katsuura Harbor. It took two years for Francis to recover from his injuries.

**6** Francis spent the next years publishing maps and guidebooks. He continued to be interested in navigation. At last, his love of the sea and sailing began to show itself. In 1953, he bought his first yacht and named it *Gipsy Moth II*. *Gipsy Moth III*, a 39-foot yacht, followed in 1959.

Francis wanted his boat to be ready for the first Trans-Atlantic Race in 1960. This race was one of the most spectacular and dangerous races for a one-man crew. Boats with full crews entered the race.

Five boats entered with only a single crew member, and Francis was one of these. He won the Single-Handed Trans-Atlantic Race. It took him 40 days in his yacht. He had had to fight head winds and gales in that time. Perhaps most amazing was that he did this while recovering from cancer.

The next year, Francis sailed solo once again across the Atlantic Ocean. He beat his earlier record by seven days. The Trans-Atlantic Race was held every four years, and Francis entered the Trans-Atlantic Race again in 1964. He sailed alone, although his boat was designed for a six-man crew. He came in second place, but he had completed the trip ten days faster than he had in 1960.

*Sir Francis Chichester with* **Gipsy Moth IV**

What was next for this sailor? Why, to sail around the world, of course! He hadn't been able to accomplish this task by plane, but he would do it by ship. Francis wanted to be the first to sail the longest route alone and he wanted to do it in the fastest time. With much help, a special boat was built: the 54-foot *Gipsy Moth IV*.

Francis's plan was to sail around Africa and across the Indian Ocean. His only stop would be in Sydney, Australia. There he would make repairs and get supplies. Next would be the longest and most dangerous part of the trip: crossing the South Pacific, rounding Cape Horn, and sailing north for England. Francis would be the first to do this solo—one man alone in a boat.

One man sailing alone means little sleep, lots of work, and many repairs. Francis battled fierce winds, huge waves, and terrible storms. At one point, the boat capsized in a tropical cyclone. Fresh water and diesel fuel ran low and food spoiled. Seasickness, food poisoning, and injuries threatened him.

The trip from Plymouth, England to Sydney, Australia was 14,100 miles. Francis made it in 107 days. Repairs in Sydney took seven weeks. Then, from there to Plymouth, he sailed another 15,517 miles in 119 days. In all, Francis sailed 29,630 miles in just 226 days! He had done what he had set out to do. The trip lasted from August 27, 1966 to May 28, 1967.

When Francis reached home, there were many celebrations. Queen Elizabeth II knighted him. She used the sword that Sir Francis Drake had given to Queen Elizabeth I almost 400 years earlier. Today, *Gipsy Moth IV* is docked on the Thames River at Greenwich, just a short distance southeast of London.

In his book *Gipsy Moth Circles the World*, Sir Francis Chichester wrote, "People keep at me about my age…. I don't think I can escape aging, but why beef about it? Our only purpose in life… is to put up the best performance we can—in anything, and only in doing so lies satisfaction in living." According to his book editor, J.R.L. Anderson, Chichester made his dreams come true: "For him, to dream is to determine, and to determine, to achieve."

Sir Francis Chichester didn't let himself get stuck in the ruts of life. At the age of 65, he achieved what no other person had yet done and few younger people would ever try! ■

1. **Why wasn't it unusual that Francis Chichester was interested in sailing?**
   A. He grew up close to the sea.
   B. He was the son of a sailor.
   C. He lived in New Zealand.
   D. He liked to fly airplanes.

   *HINT: This question asks you to think about a detail in the passage. What did the passage tell you about Francis that could explain his interest in sailing? If you are unsure of the answer, reread the beginning of the passage.*

2. **What did Francis Chichester do before any other person?**
   A. He finished the Trans-Atlantic Race.
   B. He sailed around the world by himself.
   C. He survived a shipwreck in a cyclone.
   D. He was knighted by Queen Elizabeth II.

   *HINT: This question asks you to recall a detail from the passage. If you are unsure of the answer, skim the passage, looking for a mention of something Francis was the first to do.*

3. **This passage is mostly about**
   A. the adventurous life of Francis Chichester.
   B. how Francis Chichester got over cancer.
   C. the early life of Francis Chichester.
   D. the story behind the name *Gipsy Moth.*

   *HINT: This question asks you to identify the central idea of the passage. Think about what you have read. What do you think the author was trying to tell you about?*

4. **The purpose of the seventh paragraph is to**
   A. describe Francis Chichester's participation in the first Trans-Atlantic Race.
   B. compare and contrast the *Gipsy Moth II* and the *Gipsy Moth III.*
   C. explain how Francis Chichester improved his navigation skills.
   D. discuss Francis Chichester's first attempt at sailing around the world.

   *HINT: This question also think about why the author wrote the seventh paragraph. Reread paragraph 7. What does the paragraph tell you?*

**5. Why did Francis Chichester's attempt to fly around the world fail?**

A. He did not have a seaplane.

B. He was too tired to finish.

C. He met with bad weather.

D. He crashed his airplane.

HINT: *This question asks you to recall a detail from the passage. What happened during Chichester's attempt to make a trip around the world? If you are unsure of the answer, reread the part of the passage about the trip.*

**7. What does the word "recover" mean in the sixth paragraph of the article?**

A. take back

B. relax

C. get better

D. forget about

HINT: *This question asks you to identify the meaning of the word "recover." If you are unsure of the answer, reread paragraph 5. Are there any clues to the word's meaning in the sentence the word is used in?*

**6. Where did Francis Chichester live for most of his life?**

A. New Zealand

B. Australia

C. Japan

D. England

HINT: *This question asks you to recall a detail from the passage. If you are unsure of the answer, look over the passage. You should be looking for a mention of where Chichester lived.*

**8. What was the mood in England when Francis Chichester returned on May 28, 1967?**

A. calm and relieved

B. sympathetic and pleased

C. worried and anxious

D. excited and proud

HINT: *This question asks you to recall a detail from the passage. If you are unsure of the answer, reread the part of the passage that mentions Chichester's return to England in 1967.*

**9. What is a theme of this passage?**
   A. Flying is usually very dangerous.
   B. Sailing around the world is impossible.
   C. People can live their dreams at any age.
   D. People don't know what they really want.

*HINT: This question asks you to identify the theme of the passage. What did you think after you completed reading the passage? What do you think the author was trying to say?*

**FOR THE OPEN-ENDED QUESTION BELOW, REMEMBER TO:**
- Pay attention to what the question is asking you.
- Be sure to answer everything the question asks you.
- Fully explain what you mean by your answer.
- Use details from the story/passage.

10. **If you could have gone with Sir Francis Chichester on one of his trips, which trip would you have chosen?**
   - **Name the trip you would like to have gone on with Francis Chichester.**
   - **Give at least four reasons why you chose that trip.**

   **Use information from the article to support your response.**

**FOR THE OPEN-ENDED QUESTION BELOW, REMEMBER TO:**
• Pay attention to what the question is asking you.
• Be sure to answer everything the question asks you.
• Fully explain what you mean by your answer.
• Use details from the story/passage.

11. **In the article, the author tells a lot about Sir Francis Chichester.**
    • **Write a description of Francis Chichester's character.**
    • **Tell four important things he did.**
    **Use information from the article to support your response.**

_____

_____

_____

_____

_____

_____

_____

_____

_____

_____

_____

_____

## YOU TRY IT

**DIRECTIONS**   Read the passage below and answer the questions that follow.

# A Marine Menace

Jason spends summers at his family's vacation home on the New Jersey shore. He knows a lot about the ocean and its creatures. As he returns to the beach each year, he sees the

changes brought about by winter storms. Beach erosion is a constant problem because it can cause huge amounts of sand to shift or become lost to the ocean. While Jason doesn't fear the power of the water and tides, he does respect what they can do.

Often, as Jason and his friends play along the water's edge, they find the remains of animals. Some have died as part of their life cycle. Others are victims of storms. Clam and mussel shells are everywhere. They are part of the food chain. Seagulls, terns, and other shore birds scramble ahead of incoming waves. They feast on the creatures the water leaves behind.

The animals that live in the ocean interest Jason. He finds the shore fascinating. One day last week, Jason found the shell of a horseshoe crab washed up on the beach. He took it home and soaked it for hours to remove the odor. It is now on his dresser with another one and the egg case of a skate. A skate is a large marine fish of the ray family with a flattened, diamond-shaped body.

Every day something new captures Jason's attention. From the beach, he can see the charter boats that provide whale-watching trips for visitors.

 **CHECK FOR UNDERSTANDING**

What do you think is meant by the term "the food chain"?

---

Commercial fishermen head out to sea from a nearby marina for a day of deep-sea fishing. He also sees party and private boats traveling along the ocean.

Today, as Jason is throwing a stick for his dog Pepper to fetch, he notices a group of glowing objects bobbing along on the surface of the water. As a wave brings the objects closer, Jason sees that they are small disk-shaped jellyfish. Each one is about an inch in diameter. Pepper is curious about these strange animals. He moves closer to inspect them. Jason immediately calls for Pepper to come back. Although these jellies are small, Jason knows that they could sting his dog. A sting could be very painful.

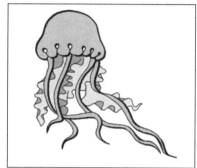

Recently, Jason saw a TV program about jellyfish. He learned that they are found in all of the oceans. There are many kinds of jellies. They go through two stages of development: the *polyp stage* and the *medusa stage*.

- In the *polyp stage*, the animal lives along the ocean floor. It is on a stem attached to seaweed or other objects.

- In its *medusa stage*, it is a free-swimming jellyfish, which are 99 percent water. Some are only an inch across. Others can be six and a half feet in diameter.

Tentacles—spaced around their outer perimeter—help jellyfish to get food. Their tentacles have barbs that fasten onto their prey. As the tentacles whip around in the water, they act as a drill, pushing a thread containing poison into the other animal. This poison paralyzes the victim's tissues and eventually kills it.

For Jason, the facts about a particular type of jellyfish–the box jellyfish–were very interesting. This species' name comes from the medusa's squared-off edges. These jellies are also known as sea wasps. They are found in the Pacific Ocean from Malaya to Queensland, Australia. Visitors to these places are supposed to ask locals if it's safe to swim in the water.

Before a box jellyfish is seen, its long tentacles can sting a person, so people need to be very careful in areas where there are jellyfish around. When a person is stung, immediate medical attention is needed. A box jellyfish sting should be treated like a snakebite. The victim may stop breathing and require artificial respiration. While awaiting an ambulance, vinegar should be poured onto the injured area without removing any of the tentacles.

There's a saying about the box jellyfish: "You are only stung once in a lifetime." This is often true. In Australia, box jellyfish cause more deaths than any other non-human **10** creature. Jason is glad this menace isn't found in New Jersey's waters. He'll settle for the little jellies and animals that inhabit his seashore. ■

1. **How does Jason feel about the shore?**
   A.  bored
   B.  afraid
   C.  fascinated
   D.  hopeful

*HINT: This question asks you to draw a conclusion based on the passage. After having read about Jason's trip to the shore, how do you think he feels about it?*

2. **What should a person do first when caring for someone who has been stung by a box jellyfish?**
   A.  wait for an ambulance
   B.  pour vinegar into the wound
   C.  remove any tentacles from the wound
   D.  seek immediate medical attention

*HINT: This question asks you to recall a detail from the passage. If you are unsure of the answer, reread the second-to-last paragraph of the passage.*

3. **What does the word "menace" mean in paragraph 10?**
   A.  animal
   B.  threat
   C.  victim
   D.  sharp

*HINT: This question asks you to identify the meaning of the word "menace." If you are unsure of the answer, reread paragraph 10. Are there any clues to the word's meaning in the sentence the word is used in?*

4. **The purpose of paragraph 9 is to**
   A.  tell the reader how to react to a box jellyfish sting.
   B.  teach the reader what happens to people after box jellyfish stings.
   C.  tell the reader how snakebites are treated.
   D.  warn the reader about the dangers of box jellyfish stings.

*HINT: This question asks why the author wrote the ninth paragraph. Reread paragraph 9. What does the paragraph tell you?*

**5. Why does Jason call for Pepper to come back?**
   A. Pepper is very small.
   B. Pepper can't swim.
   C. Pepper is learning to fetch.
   D. Pepper might get stung.

HINT: *This question asks about a detail from the passage. For what reason would Jason call for Pepper to come back? If you are unsure of the answer, reread the fifth paragraph.*

**7. What is this passage mostly about?**
   A. a boy who learns about jellyfish
   B. a boy and his dog at the beach
   C. a jellyfish that is harmful to people
   D. a family's home on the seashore

HINT: *This question asks you to identify the central idea of the passage. Think about what you have read. What do you think the author was trying to tell you about?*

**6. How does Jason learn about box jellyfish?**
   A. by reading about them
   B. by watching them
   C. by watching television
   D. by talking to others

HINT: *This question asks you to recall a detail from the passage. If you are unsure of the answer, reread the part of the story that talks about box jellyfish.*

**FOR THE OPEN-ENDED QUESTION BELOW, REMEMBER TO:**
• Pay attention to what the question is asking you.
• Be sure to answer everything the question asks you.
• Fully explain what you mean by your answer.
• Use details from the story/passage.

8. This passage describes many things about jellyfish.
   • Briefly describe the two stages of development of a jellyfish.
   Use information from the passage to support your response.

**FOR THE OPEN-ENDED QUESTION BELOW, REMEMBER TO:**
• Pay attention to what the question is asking you.
• Be sure to answer everything the question asks you.
• Fully explain what you mean by your answer.
• Use details from the story/passage.

9. Jellyfish have a unique way of catching their food.
    • **Describe the uses of a jellyfish's tentacles.**
    **Use information from the passage to support your response.**

## YOU TRY IT

| **DIRECTIONS** | Read this passage and answer the questions that follow. |
| **INTRODUCTION** | Some animals get a reputation that they do not deserve. Read this story to learn about one of these animals. |

# Gila Monsters *(Pronunciation: Gila = HE-la)*

A Gila monster is one of only two poisonous lizards in the world. Gila monsters live in the deserts of Mexico and in the southwestern United States. Their name comes from the place where they were first found, the Gila Basin in Arizona.

Actually, the Gila monster is not a monster at all. It is a stout-bodied lizard with short legs and a short, fat tail. When fully grown, Gilas measure up to 24 inches long and weigh between three and five pounds. They can live for as long as 20 years.

Almost anyone can identify a Gila monster. Its skin is black with contrasting pink, yellow, or orange stripes and spots. The bright colors warn other animals to stay away; and that's good for the other animals because the Gila is poisonous. It has no natural enemies.

Few people ever see a Gila monster in the wild. They are inactive most of the time because of the heat of their habitat. In fact, they spend fewer than two weeks per year above ground. They prefer to live under the ground in burrows. Sometimes they will steal other animals' burrows. Other times, they will

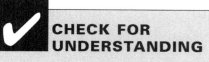

**CHECK FOR UNDERSTANDING**

What does a Gila monster look like? Would you be able to identify one? Why or why not?

dig their own. Gila monsters also have excellent hearing and vision. This allows them to lie inside a burrow and wait until any nearby intruder is gone.

Gilas are slow-moving, shy, and retiring. However, they can be dangerous when cornered. When threatened, they will first look for a burrow in which to escape. If no burrows are nearby, the Gila will turn and inflate its body, hiss loudly, and open its mouth wide. It wants to scare away its attacker. A Gila will only bite if it is unable to get away. If it does bite, it does not generally let go until the other animal is no longer a threat. If it bites a person, the Gila needs to be pulled off. A Gila monster will usually only bite a human if it is picked up.

These animals do not inject their venom like snakes. Their poison is in a different kind of saliva gland. When a Gila bites, it will often leave a half-inch-deep wound. As it is hanging onto the person or animal, the venom flows into the wound through the animal's hollow lower teeth. The Gila may even chew or tear the flesh to allow more poison to enter the wound. Gila venom is about as toxic as a rattlesnake's venom. However, only a small amount ever gets into a person or animal's body.

At one time, this lizard was widely feared because it is poisonous. Many interesting myths sprang up about the Gila. The most unusual one was that the breath of a Gila monster could poison a person. People were afraid that this would happen even if they **7** just saw one in the desert. In truth, a person bitten by a Gila will feel severe pain in 30 seconds. Swelling, chills, and weakness will follow. The bite will not be fatal to most people. Myths about Gilas killing many people are not true.

A Gila prefers to eat eggs for food. It will also eat young rodents and small animals. Gilas can climb into low bushes looking for food. They use their sharp, short claws when climbing. They prefer, however, to stay on the ground in search of food. Gila **8** monsters can eat huge amounts of food at one time and then store the fat in their tails and bodies. Gilas hibernate in the winter. During this time, they live off the fat stored in their tails.

Gila monsters mate in July and lay three to fifteen eggs a few weeks later. The eggs are buried in the hot sand. They will hatch about a month later. When born, the babies are three to four inches long. They can survive on their own after they hatch. By the time they are three years old, Gila monsters have reached adult size.

The number of Gila monsters living in the wild is becoming fewer each year. The problem is that their habitat is being destroyed by human development. Gila monsters are a protected species under Arizona state law in the United States. They may not be killed or kept in captivity without a license there. They are listed as a threatened species under the United States Federal Endangered Species Act in this country, and are also endangered in Mexico.

If you live in an area where Gila monsters might live, keep an eye out. Even though you may not see them, you can still help to preserve their privacy and their way of life. ■

1. **Why do people think Gila monsters are dangerous?**
   A. They are very fast.
   B. They have very bright colors.
   C. They are poisonous.
   D. They have many natural enemies.

   *HINT: This question asks you to draw a conclusion based on the passage. What about Gila monsters would make people think they are dangerous?*

2. **What does the word "fatal" mean in paragraph 7?**
   A. deep
   B. deadly
   C. scary
   D. painful

   *HINT: This question asks you to identify the meaning of the word "fatal." If you are unsure of the answer, reread the seventh paragraph. Are there any clues to the word's meaning in the sentence the word is used in?*

3. **Why are there fewer Gila monsters living in the wild each year?**
   A. Gila monsters can be trapped and traded or sold without a permit.
   B. Gila monsters' habitat is being destroyed by human development.
   C. Gila monsters' hearing and vision are not very good.
   D. Gila monsters cannot defend themselves against other animals.

   *HINT: This question asks you to draw a conclusion based on the passage. If you are unsure of the answer, reread the last two paragraphs of the passage.*

4. **Why do few people ever see Gila monsters in the wild?**
   A. Gila monsters are only active when it is very cold outside.
   B. Gila monsters spend most of their time in trees and prefer to climb.
   C. Gila monsters are endangered and are mostly found in captivity.
   D. Gila monsters spend less than two weeks per year above ground.

   *HINT: This question asks you to draw a conclusion based on the passage. Which answer best explains why few people would see Gila monsters?*

**5. Why might a Gila monster attack a person?**
   A. because Gila monsters are very aggressive and dangerous
   B. because Gila monsters mistake people for enemies
   C. because the person tries to pick up the Gila monster
   D. because the person threatens the Gila monster's habitat

HINT: *This question asks you to draw a conclusion based on the passage. If you are unsure of the answer, reread the fifth paragraph.*

**6. The purpose of the eighth paragraph is to**
   A. tell readers about the eating habits of Gila monsters.
   B. inform readers that Gila monsters are very dangerous.
   C. explain why people rarely see Gila monsters.
   D. describe what Gila monsters look like.

HINT: *This question asks you to think about why the author wrote the eighth paragraph. Reread paragraph 8. What does the paragraph tell you?*

**7. What is this passage mostly about?**
   A. It explains why Gila monsters are dangerous.
   B. It describes the laws that protect the Gila monster.
   C. It describes Gila monsters and how they live in the wild.
   D. It explains what has been done to protect the Gila monster.

HINT: *This question asks you to identify the central idea of the passage. Think about what you have read. What do you think the author was trying to tell you about?*

**8. What does the word "prefer" mean in paragraph 8?**
   A. likes
   B. hates
   C. forgets
   D. refuses

HINT: *This question asks you to identify the meaning of the word "prefer." If you are unsure of the answer, reread the eighth paragraph. Are there any clues to the word's meaning in the sentence the word is used in?*

**FOR THE OPEN-ENDED QUESTION BELOW, REMEMBER TO:**
• Pay attention to what the question is asking you.
• Be sure to answer everything the question asks you.
• Fully explain what you mean by your answer.
• Use details from the story/passage.

9. Gila monsters rarely bite people; however, it does happen occasionally if, for example, one is picked up.
   • **Describe how a Gila monster bites.**
   • **Then describe what happens after it strikes a person.**
   **Use information from the article to support your response.**

## YOU TRY IT

| | |
|---|---|
| **DIRECTIONS INTRODUCTION** | Read this story/passage and answer the questions that follow. When the name "Viking" is mentioned, many people think of fighting and raiding. Few people know that the Vikings did more farming and trading than raiding and fighting. This passage tells what the Vikings were really like. |

# The Vikings

**Background**

The period from 800 to 1100 c.e. is called the Viking Age. Most people think of it as a time when the Vikings raided all over Europe. It was thought that no town along the coast was safe.

However, this picture of the Vikings is beginning to change. It is true that they did attack and destroy many towns. However, we now know that most Vikings lived and worked as farmers. Many of them were also good traders.

In fact, the Vikings traded more than they raided. Viking ships sailed all over the known world to trade. The Vikings also discovered new lands in their travels, including Iceland, Greenland, and parts of North America. Some of the towns settled by Vikings still exist today.

**CHECK FOR UNDERSTANDING**

Why do you think most people thought of Vikings as dangerous?

These people lived in northern Europe. They were mostly farmers who went sailing in the summer. Their name comes from the word, "Vik." This was the name of a pirate center in southern Norway at this time.

Vikings went on raiding parties, called "a-viking." Later, this was shortened to "Viking".

**The Vikings as Raiders**

The Viking Age started with an attack on England in the late 700s. On a sunny day, Vikings attacked a monastery and destroyed the buildings and took the church's treasure.

This attack was the first of many in England, Scotland, and Ireland. In the early 800s, the attacks spread to Europe, and the Viking Age was born. Eventually, Viking attacks were occurring all over the known world. However, the Vikings did not attack all the time.

*Figure 1*

Attacks occurred when the men in a Viking village decided to do some raiding after spring planting. The men would sail away in their longboats looking for villages to attack. Near the end of the summer, the men would return to help with the harvest. There were years when no Viking attacks were recorded.

Rarely did large numbers of Vikings make a raid. Most Viking attacks were conducted by small groups of men. They used anywhere from two to ten ships with about thirty raiders on each ship. The ships would suddenly appear offshore. (*Figure 1* shows Vikings preparing to attack a coastal town.)

The Vikings would attack before the village could organize a defense. The battle would end quickly.

Then the Vikings would retreat before help arrived. They took their treasure and captives away on the ships. The town would then be burned before they left.

People had two names for these Viking pirates. They were called either "Norsemen" or "Northmen" because they came from the north.

The term "Viking", which is used today, was not actually used until long after the Viking Age ended in 1100 c.e.

The Vikings enjoyed fighting; they were bold, fierce warriors. Most fought with two-bladed swords or axes, but they also used bows and arrows or spears. Each man also carried a wooden shield and many wore some sort of armor.

Most armor was made from animal hides. Only important men had metal armor. Viking helmets were plain and did not have horns on the sides, which you may see in illustrations or movies.

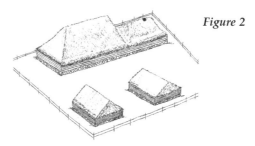

*Figure 2*

## Vikings as Farmers

Most Vikings lived on small farms. These farms were often clustered into small villages. All Viking farms were built in the same pattern. The main building was called the "longhouse," and it could be over 100 feet long. In the early farms, the family and the animals used to share one building. Later farms had buildings around the longhouse. One of the outbuildings was always a barn, called a "byre," where the animals spent the winter.

Other buildings stored grain and meat over the winter. A fence always enclosed the buildings. Larger farms even had a blacksmith shop. (*Figure 2* shows a typical Viking farm.)

Spring was a busy time on the farm. Fields were plowed and crops planted. Vegetables were planted inside the fence. Wheat and other grains were planted in the fields outside the fence. Animals grazed in some of the fields outside the fence.

When the spring work was done, the farmer would often go raiding or trading. The Viking wives and children ran the farm. In the autumn, when everyone was needed to harvest the crops, the men would return to the farm.

Clothes and other household goods were made during the winter. Tools and equipment were crafted and repaired. The Vikings also repaired their boats during the winter months.

## Vikings as Traders

The Vikings were good traders. Sometimes they would settle in an area after the battles were over. They would build towns and bring their families. Within a short time, the Vikings would start to trade with the local people. Over time, trade increased. The trade goods were shipped to the Vikings' homeland.

Soon, many Vikings realized it was easier to trade than to fight. They started to sail to towns just to trade, bringing goods from Scandinavia. They would take other things back to their homeland. They even traveled into present-day Russia. They also traded around the Mediterranean. Viking traders became wealthy men. (*Figure 3* shows Viking trading routes.)

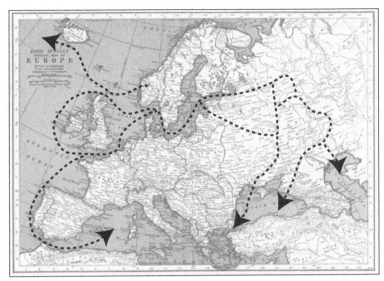

*Figure 3*

Once trading began, attacks lessened. The Vikings learned that there was more money in peace than in war. By the late 900s, Vikings preferred to trade rather than to attack towns. Many Viking centers grew into present-day cities. Kiev in Russia, Dublin in Ireland, and York, England were all once Viking trading centers.

**Vikings as Sailors**

The Vikings were the best sailors of their time. In the late 800s, some Vikings began to sail across the Atlantic Ocean. They sailed in open ships in all types of weather at a time when most sailors played it safe by staying nearer to land. During some of these voyages, Vikings found new lands. Vikings were the first to see Iceland, Greenland, and parts of North America. Colonies were started in all three. Only the colony in North America was not successful. After three years, it was abandoned.

**Summary**

The Viking Age lasted about 300 years. By 1060 c.e., the Vikings were living in peace with their neighbors.

Many important things came from the Viking Age. Trade between countries increased and the nations of Norway, Sweden, and Denmark were formed. Countries in Europe became stronger as they fought off the Viking attacks. Iceland was found and settled. Even the use of law as a way to settle disputes came from the Vikings. ■

**1. How does the author most likely feel about the Vikings? He thinks**

    A. The Viking Age meant one raid after another.

    B. The Vikings were not really good fighters.

    C. The Vikings were more than just raiders.

    D. The Vikings were a peaceful people.

*HINT: This question asks you to make a judgment based on the passage. If you are unsure of the answer, look in the passage for hints of the author's opinion.*

**2. Why did Vikings stop raiding people?**

    A. They began to get in trouble.

    B. They made more money by trading.

    C. They started to feel sorry for others.

    D. They wanted to be welcomed at places.

*HINT: This question asks you to recall a detail from the passage. What motivated the Vikings to stop raiding? If you are unsure of the answer, reread the second half of the passage.*

**3. Read this sentence from the passage.**

*Eventually*, Viking attacks were occurring all over the known world.

**What does the word "eventually" mean in this sentence?**

    A. generally

    B. daringly

    C. casually

    D. finally

*HINT: This question asks you to identify the meaning of the word "eventually." Are there any clues to the word's meaning in the sentence?*

**4. Why did the Viking men usually return home near the end of the summer?**

    A. to harvest the crops

    B. to trade their goods

    C. to rebuild the barn

    D. to repair their boats

*HINT: This question asks you to think about a detail from the passage. For what reason would the Viking men return home at the end of the summer? If you are unsure of the answer, skim the passage.*

**5. The purpose of the headings in bold print is to**
   A. make finding information easier.
   B. remind readers what they're reading.
   C. tell what the Vikings liked to be called.
   D. show that the Vikings had many names.

*HINT: This question asks you to think about why the author included bold headings. Did the headings help you as a reader? How?*

**6. Read the following sentence from the passage.**
   By the late 900s, Vikings *preferred* to trade rather than to attack towns.
   **What does the word "preferred" mean?**
   A. urged
   B. wanted
   C. swore
   D. hinted

*HINT: This question asks you to identify the meaning of the word "preferred." Are there any clues to the word's meaning in the sentence?*

**7. What is this article mostly about?**
   A. the Viking Age
   B. Viking attacks
   C. what Vikings traded
   D. Viking families

*HINT: This question asks you to identify the central idea of the passage. Think about what you have read. What do you think the author was trying to tell you about?*

**8. The purpose of the introduction to this article is to**
   A. explain what the word "Viking" means.
   B. prove that kind people raid sometimes.
   C. tell readers what the article is about.
   D. show readers when the Vikings lived.

*HINT: This question asks you to think about why the author included bold headings. Did the headings help you as a reader? How?*

**9. Why were the Vikings most likely able to find new lands?**

   A. They scared people from their homes.

   B. Most people did not think there were other lands.

   C. They sailed very far away from their homeland.

   D. Most people wanted to share land with the Vikings.

*HINT: This question asks you to draw a conclusion based on the passage. Was there something that Vikings thought or did that gave them access to new lands?*

**10. Why did the author most likely write this passage?**

   A. to show why the Vikings acted the way they did

   B. to show in detail how Vikings fought with others

   C. to teach about places where the Vikings lived

   D. to teach about what the Vikings were really like

*HINT: This question asks you to make a judgment based on the passage. What do you think the author's goal was in writing this passage?*

**FOR THE OPEN-ENDED QUESTION BELOW, REMEMBER TO:**
- Pay attention to what the question is asking you.
- Be sure to answer everything the question asks you.
- Fully explain what you mean by your answer.
- Use details from the story/passage.

11. Describe the life of a Viking living on a farm in Scandinavia. Use information from the article to support your response.

# CHAPTER 2

# Understanding Text
## Vocabulary and a Purpose for Reading

**RL.5.4; RI.5.4; RF.5.3: DETERMINE MEANING**
**RL.5.10; RI.5.10: READ AND COMPREHEND**

Reading can be fun and it can also be challenging. As you grow in your mastery of the skills of reading, you will hopefully get more out of what you read. You may find yourself looking forward to each challenge and approaching reading exercises on the Common Core Language Arts Test with more confidence.

When it comes to taking tests, make sure to think carefully about what you are reading. If you do this, you will more quickly recognize when there is a new word within the text. You may already know that you can try to determine the meaning of each new word by studying the words around it—the **context clues**.

## YOU TRY IT

You have just finished reading a story. You saw a word with which you were not familiar. What do you do now?

- Do you look the word up in a dictionary right away?
- Do you try to guess what the new word means by rereading the paragraph?

When taking a test, you won't have the opportunity to use a dictionary to look up a new word. Your best strategy in that situation would be to use context clues to give you hints as you try to discover the word's meaning.

## RL.5.4; RI.5.4; RF.5.3: DETERMINE MEANING

### What does "context clues" mean?

The words and sentences around a word are the **context**.

To really understand what is being said or written, you have to know the context—the facts, the circumstances, the setting, the events, or even the tone of the situation.

A **clue** is something that helps to solve a problem.

Anything you find in what you are reading—including the facts, the circumstances, the setting, the events, or even the tone—can be clues that may be helpful in determining what an unfamiliar word means.

### So, what are context clues?

The sentences, phrases, and words that are around an unfamiliar word are **context clues**.

The challenge is to find the meaning of the new word. So, the context clues help you to find the meaning of the new word.

Sometimes just reading the paragraph again and looking at the words around the new word will let you know what it means.

## How do I use context clues?

Read this sentence for an example of the use of context clues.

> After working very hard for months, the students had raised enough money to help their sick friend get a new *blossingter*.

What is a *blossingter*?

A *blossingter* is just a made-up word. Nevertheless, you can tell from the words "money" and "sick"— the context clues— that a *blossingter* is probably some kind of expensive medical aid or perhaps an organ of the body.

## Now it's your turn!

Here's one for you to try:

*Zelicrafting* the heavy rains, the small town prepared to avoid the threat of flooding.

What is *zelicrafting*? Write your guesses below.

_____

_____

Which words in the sentence gave you clues? Write your guesses below.

_____

_____

## Could the same word have two meanings?

Have you ever read a word that you thought you knew, only to realize that the word meaning you knew did not fit into the sentence?

This could be the case if the word has **more than one meaning**.

The same word could have even more than two meanings. As you've probably discovered by now, some words can be used in many different ways.

## What do I do if I come upon a word with more than one meaning?

When this happens, a dictionary would be the best resource to use to find out which meaning of the word makes the most sense.

However, when taking a test, using a dictionary is not an option.

So during a test, it is best for you to think about what you know about the context clues in the sentence to determine what the word means.

## How can I tell which meaning is being used?

Here are a dictionary entry and sample sentences for
a word with multiple meanings.

**bark** [bärk]
1. (verb)  to make the cry of a dog or a similar sound
2. (verb)  to speak in a harsh, scolding tone
3. (noun)  the outside covering of the stems and roots
   of plants
4. (noun)  candy, usually chocolate with large pieces of
   nuts, made in flat sheets

**Example using definition 1**
Oreo, my cousin's dog, likes to bark too much.

**Example using definition 2**
In the summer when the windows are open, we can hear our neighbor barking at his
children.

**Example using definition 3**
The scout leader took us on a winter hike and, just by looking at the bark, could
identify all the trees we saw along the way.

**Example using definition 4**
I like buttercreams, but Mina's favorite is almond bark.

## What if different words sound the same?

Words that sound the same but are spelled differently are called **homonyms**.

How will you be able to identify words that are pronounced and/or spelled the same, but have different meanings?

There are some very simple words that can be confusing to read and confusing to use when you write.

Let's begin with a set of words that sound alike but have different spellings and uses: **there, they're**, and **their**. These are not difficult words, but they are often confused.

---

**there**
position; in or at that place; and toward, or into that place.

---

**they're**
contraction of "they are."
[HINT: In a contraction, the apostrophe indicates that letters are missing.]

---

**their**
belonging or relating to them. It is the possessive of "they" and describes a noun.

---

**Example using *there***
*There* is no reason for Tad to stay. He has finished the job.

**Example using *they're***
Where are Colleen and Sarah? *They're* outside.

**Example using *their***
I've met them before, but I don't know *their* names.

---

## LET'S TRY IT TOGETHER

| **DIRECTIONS** For each sentence, put the correct word in the blank. |
| --- |

**there**    **they're**    **their**

1. _____ are several mistakes in this article. I'm going to rewrite it.

2. I'm starving! Are _____ any more honey-roasted cashews left?

3. My aunt and uncle have put their house up for sale because the neighbors are too noisy. They play loud music until 3:00 a.m. and, after that, _____ dog barks until the sun comes up.

4. "Don't touch the cookies I just baked!" warned Mrs. Lopez. "_____ for the church bake sale."

5. Because my careless little brother Wade is always dripping cranberry juice, you'll notice spots here and _____ on the dining room rug.

6. Despite complaints from his parents, Ned continues to wear his dirty, old, smelly sneakers because_____ the most comfortable shoes he has.

7. Even though it was the rule, Kelly and Tamara came to English class without _____ dictionaries. Mr. Schmidt, their teacher, was so displeased that he gave them extra work to do.

**RL.5.10; RI.5.10: READ AND COMPREHEND**

## What is the reader's purpose for reading?

A **reader's purpose** is the reason why a reader reads something.

Readers set different purposes, or goals, before and when they are reading.

You might read a comic strip or silly story to be entertained. You might read an encyclopedia or dictionary entry to learn something new about a topic.

As readers, we must set a purpose, or reason, to read something before we read it.

## How do I set a purpose for reading?

Before you read a passage, preview the title, illustrations and headings to figure out what you might learn from reading it.

Ask yourself questions like:

- "Why do I want to read this?"
- "What will I learn from reading this?"
- "When would I want to read this?"

Readers read for a number of reasons. Setting a purpose for reading will help you understand the story or passage and remember what you have read.

**Try to list all of the different reasons why you might read something.**

**List what you would read to be entertained; to learn something new; to follow directions.**

## What is an author's purpose for writing?

An **author's purpose** is the reason why an author has written a particular story or text.

Every author has a purpose, or reason, for writing what she or he has written. Some common reasons why people choose to write are to **inform**, to **persuade**, to **teach**, or to **entertain**.

## What is the author's purpose?

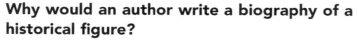

**Why would an author write a biography of a historical figure?**
Authors of biographies usually want to inform readers about the life of a particular person.

**What would an author write directions for making a pinhole camera?**
Instructions and recipes are written to teach readers to make or to do something.

**Why would an author write about why it is necessary to get a good education?**
The author would most likely want to persuade readers of the value of education and of the opportunities it opens up in a person's life.

When you are reading, remember to think about what the author's purpose was in writing the text. This will help you better understand what you read!

## LET'S TRY IT TOGETHER

**DIRECTIONS**   Read the story/passage and together we will discuss the questions.

# The X Prize

Have you heard about the X PRIZE? An X PRIZE is a multi-million-dollar award given to the first team to achieve a specific goal, a goal with the potential to benefit humanity. The members of the X PRIZE Foundation set the goals as they try to stimulate new inventions that will make life better for everyone on Earth.

On October 4, 2004, the Mojave Aerospace Ventures team, led by famed aircraft designer Burt Rutan and financed by Microsoft co-founder Paul Allen, captured the Ansari X PRIZE. The world took notice of this great achievement and the winning SpaceShipOne is now hanging in the Smithsonian National Air & Space Museum.

The X PRIZE Foundation's founder and chief executive officer, Peter Diamandis, has just issued a worldwide challenge for teams to come up with an efficient car model that can be mass-produced. Teams will have about a year and a half to build their vehicles before the first qualifying race in 2009.

Would you like to be part of an X PRIZE team one day?

## What was the author's purpose for writing this story?

**Was it to persuade readers to join a team working to win the X PRIZE?**
No, that is not the author's purpose in this article. The author does not try to convince readers that they should try to be part of a group competing for an X PRIZE.

**Was it to explain to readers how to apply for the X PRIZE?**
No, that is also not the author's purpose in the article. While the article gives information about the X PRIZE, it does not tell readers how to get involved themselves.

**Was it to entertain readers by telling about an unusual prize?**
No, that is also not the author's purpose. The article tells readers about this prize and it is factual, but not really entertaining.

**Was it to inform readers about this unique prize?**
Yes, that is the author's purpose. The article informs readers about awards given to teams who, working together, achieve certain goals intended to benefit humanity.

When you are reading, ask yourself why the author has written what you are reading. If you remember to ask yourself several times while reading the passage, the hints about the author's purpose may be easier to see.

## YOU TRY IT

| DIRECTIONS INTRODUCTION | Read this passage and answer the questions that follow. The National Park System is responsible for overseeing special areas in the United States. These areas include sights and places that are unusual and/or related to our national history. This passage tells about the National Park System. |
|---|---|

# National Parks

When people first came to America, they did not think about preserving land for the future. They thought that all the land should be used for any purpose. Trees were cut down to build homes. Fields were cleared to farm. People changed the land for their own needs. They did not see forests as beautiful things that needed preserving. They felt that there was plenty of land for everyone to use as they pleased.

The Fairy Tale Trail, seen above, is located in Utah and is part of Bryce National Park.

By the 1800s, most people lived in the eastern United States. Here there were many towns, cities, and roads. Farms dotted the lands in this area. Unlike the east coast region, the part of the United States west of the Mississippi River still had open land. There the towns and farms were farther apart from one another.

People began to spread stories about the wonders in the west. Trappers told about things never seen in the east. At first people on the east coast thought these were tall tales. However, as newspapers and books began to tell stories about unusual sights, people finally began believing the tales.

In the 1850s, people started discussing whether or not to set aside land for people to enjoy in the future. Something had to be done before these sights were lost, some argued. If they were destroyed, future generations would never get to see these wonders.

An area called "Wonderland" in the Rocky Mountains was the first of these areas to be saved. It was along the upper Yellowstone River. People had known about this area's wonders since Lewis and Clark's expedition.

Later, trappers confirmed that these wonders existed. They said that hot water shot hundreds of feet into the air. There were rainbow-colored pools of water and unusual rock formations everywhere. Today, we call this area Yellowstone National Park.

In 1872, Yellowstone became a national park. Congress said it was to be kept forever as a public park for people's enjoyment. It was the first park of its kind in the world.

The army oversaw the park. Unfortunately, while they do a good job of protecting the people, they didn't do such a good job of managing the park. At the same time, few people then knew much about wildlife management and conservation.

In the early 1900s, the number of areas within the Park System grew. Some parks came from land donated by states. The government bought other land with special sights for parks. Four more national parks were formed.

The parks had some problems. More visitors started to come to them, but many of these people were careless. They destroyed the area and left trash everywhere. Buildings were put up that then blocked the sights people had come to see. People were destroying much of the parks' scenery and natural beauty. Clearly something needed to be done before the parks that were being set aside for future generations were ruined.

**CHECK FOR UNDERSTANDING**

What do you know about wildlife management and conservation?

In 1916, Congress decided to act. They created the National Park Service. Its job was to regulate the use of the parks and to protect the parks' scenery and natural beauty. Right away the Park Service passed rules protecting the parks. Park rangers enforced these rules. The Park Service removed the buildings that blocked the beautiful views. It tried to preserve as much of each park's wilderness as possible.

Today, there are over 360 special places in the National Park System. They fall into various groups, such as national parks and monuments. There are also historical sites, recreation areas, parkways, and scenic trails.

The Park Service tries to keep each area as close to its natural state as possible. However, over the years, this has become more difficult. The parks face many problems. The main problem is tourists. The number of park visitors continues to increase. Often there are too many people for the size of the park. Some parks now limit the number of people allowed to visit their sites.

No one knows the future of our parks. We need to do what we can to protect them. It is important to preserve these wonders for future generations. ∎

*The Udine Falls are located in Wyoming and are part of Yellowstone National Park. Figure 1*

**1. Why did the author most likely write this passage?**
   A. to encourage people to open parks
   B. to describe a visit to a national park
   C. to encourage people to protect parks
   D. to describe how the first explorers found parks

*HINT: This question asks you to determine the author's purpose. If you are unsure of the answer, skim the passage looking for the author's purpose.*

**2. What was one difference between the eastern and western United States according to this passage?**
   A. The eastern region had more factories, while the western region had most of the farmlands.
   B. The western region was more developed, while the eastern region had most of the unusual sights.
   C. The western region included more unusual sights, while the eastern region had more open land.
   D. The eastern region was more developed, while the western region had more open land.

*HINT: This question asks you to think about a detail from the passage. What did the passage say about the differences between the eastern and western parts of the U.S.? If you are unsure of the answer, reread the beginning of the passage.*

**3. Which sentence best summarizes the passage?**
   A. The best national park is located in the Rocky Mountains.
   B. People who don't like national parks should reconsider going there.
   C. Parks are a great way to make lots of money from people.
   D. Parks will allow future generations to see special places.

*HINT: This question asks you to describe the passage in one sentence. Of the answer options, which best captures what the author was trying to say?*

**4. Read the following sentence from the passage.**
   "Its job was to *regulate* the use of the parks and to protect the parks' scenery and natural beauty."
   **What does the word "regulate" mean in this sentence?**
   A. discuss
   B. visit
   C. manage
   D. clean

*HINT: This question asks you to identify the meaning of the word "regulate." Are there any clues to the word's meaning in the sentence?*

     Explore CCSS/PARCC Grade 5 Reading

**5. The article "National Parks" would be useful in learning**

  A.  how and why the National Park System was started.

  B.  about the first three national parks in the United States.

  C.  why Yellowstone is not special among national parks.

  D.  what the reader can do to protect the national parks.

*HINT: This question asks you to think about the passage. What more could you learn from the text? If you are unsure of the answer, skim the passage.*

**6. What is the area once known as "Wonderland" now called?**

  A.  Trappertown

  B.  Mississippi River

  C.  Rocky Mountains

  D.  Yellowstone National Park

*HINT: This question asks you to recall a detail from the passage. If you are unsure of the answer, look over the passage. You should be looking for a mention of "Wonderland."*

**FOR THE OPEN-ENDED QUESTION BELOW, REMEMBER TO:**
• Pay attention to what the question is asking you.
• Be sure to answer everything the question asks you.
• Fully explain what you mean by your answer.
• Use details from the story/passage.

7. An author's purpose may sometimes be to make a reader feel a certain way while reading his or her writing.
   • Briefly describe the tone and language used in this passage.
   • What do you think the tone and language used say about the author's purpose for writing the passage?
   Use information from the article to support your response.

## YOU TRY IT

| DIRECTIONS INTRODUCTION | Read this story/passage and answer the questions that follow. This is the tale of the two tiger sharks. One is very dangerous to humans and the other has never been known to attack people. |
| --- | --- |

# The Two Tiger Sharks

The word "tiger" is used for the name of two sharks: the tiger shark and the sand tiger shark. While they share almost the same name, they are drastically different.

The tiger shark is a large shark that can grow up to 20 feet in length. Most, however, are in the 10- to 14-foot range. They are similar in size to white sharks and just as deadly. However, what makes these sharks so dangerous is that they are curious and will eat anything. Tiger sharks have excellent hearing and good vision. They are always on the lookout for anything that is moving in the ocean. When they sense something in the water, they will swim right toward it.

Sharks will usually only attack people if they are provoked. With the tiger shark, however, anything is fair game. The shark typically will eat a moving object once it locates it. It's never clear whether or not the shark will ignore what it sees moving or if it is likely to take a bite out of it. Its food ranges from turtles to birds to other sharks and fish. This shark will even eat things like car tires, nails, and license plates.

Tiger sharks earned this name because of the tiger-like markings on their back. These stripes are most noticeable on younger tigers. When the sharks reach adulthood, the stripes are very faint.

The snout and teeth of a tiger shark are different from those of other sharks. Their heads are wedge-shaped and they have blunt snouts. These features allow the tiger sharks to make very fast turns while swimming.

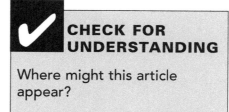

**CHECK FOR UNDERSTANDING**

Where might this article appear?

Tiger sharks also use their blunt snouts to push their prey down to the sea floor where they will crush it. Then they eat it at their leisure. Both their top and bottom teeth can be used to cut up their prey. Most other sharks only use their bottom teeth to grab and hold their prey. One time, the complete head of a crocodile was found in the stomach of a tiger shark!

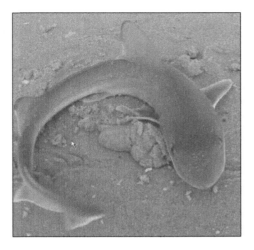

Tiger sharks are found almost worldwide in tropical and moderate salt water. They tend to swim in deep water during the day. However, they have been known to come close to shore to feed at dusk or at night.

The sand tiger shark, on the other hand, is quite different from the tiger shark. For one thing, it is considerably smaller, growing to be between four and eight feet in length. The largest it will grow is to a length of 11 feet.

Also, sand tigers look more threatening than they actually are. These sharks have a short, flat snout and a stout body. They have three rows of narrow, curved teeth. Their teeth are always visible because the sand tiger swims with its mouth open. The shark sheds its teeth about every two weeks. New teeth come in at the same time the other teeth are falling out.

Despite their frightening appearance, these sharks are generally harmless. Divers can approach them without fear. Sand tigers are also shy and tend to swim away when approached. These sharks are also unique in the way they maintains their buoyancy. Sand tigers will swim to the surface and swallow air before they submerge. This enables them to move around under water and stay at any depth they want. Although strong, these sharks tend to swim slowly.

Sand tiger sharks are found all over the world in moderate climates. Interestingly, they are not found in Caribbean waters. These sharks, unfortunately, have been hunted almost to extinction. Today, sand tiger sharks are on the protected list. ■

1. **What causes tiger sharks to be so dangerous to humans?**
   A. They are very shy and easily frightened.
   B. They are curious and will eat anything.
   C. They are very small and difficult to see.
   D. They use only their bottom teeth to grab and hold prey.

*HINT: This question asks you to recall a detail from the passage. What makes tiger sharks so dangerous? If you are unsure of the answer, reread the beginning of the passage.*

2. **How are tiger sharks different from sand tiger sharks?**
   A. Tiger sharks live in cool climates, and sand tiger sharks live in very warm climates.
   B. Tiger sharks are harmless, and sand tiger sharks are dangerous.
   C. Tiger sharks are somewhat small, and sand tiger sharks are very large.
   D. Tiger sharks are interested in everything, and sand tiger sharks are shy.

*HINT: This question asks you to draw a conclusion based on the passage. How do the two types of tiger sharks differ?*

3. **Why are sand tiger sharks on the protected list?**
   A. They are not harmful to humans.
   B. There is not enough food to feed them.
   C. They must swallow air before swimming.
   D. There are not many of them left.

*HINT: This question asks you to think about information from the passage. For what reason would sand tiger sharks be on the protected list?*

4. **This passage is mostly about**
   A. differences between tiger sharks and sand tiger sharks.
   B. funny stories about tiger sharks and sand tiger sharks.
   C. the foods that tiger sharks and sand tiger sharks like to eat.
   D. the areas where tiger sharks and sand tiger sharks are found.

*HINT: This question asks you to identify the central idea of the passage. Which answer best describes the passage?*

**5. Read the following sentences.**

"Tiger sharks also use their blunt snouts
to push their prey down to the sea floor
where they will crush it. Then they eat
it at their leisure."

**What does the word "leisure" mean?**

A. hardship

B. caution

C. convenience

D. dwelling

*HINT: This question asks you to identify the meaning of the word "leisure." Are there any clues to the word's meaning in the sentence?*

**6. Why did the author most likely write this passage?**

A. to inform readers about a very
dangerous shark

B. to tell readers about two types of
sharks with similar names

C. to teach readers how to identify
many different types of sharks

D. to convince readers not to approach
two types of sharks

*HINT: This question asks you to think about the passage. Why do you think the author decided to write this passage?*

**FOR THE OPEN-ENDED QUESTION BELOW, REMEMBER TO:**
- Pay attention to what the question is asking you.
- Be sure to answer everything the question asks you.
- Fully explain what you mean by your answer.
- Use details from the story/passage.

7. The tiger shark and the sand tiger shark have similar names, but they are very different.
   - **Contrast these two kinds of sharks, being sure to point out how they are different.**
   - **Include at least three differences between these two sharks.**

   **Use information from the article to support your response.**

## YOU TRY IT

**DIRECTIONS**   Read the passage below and answer the questions that follow.

# Conduct Code for Midland School

**Student Code of Conduct**

Students are expected to know the contents of the Code of Conduct. These rules apply to all things pertaining to the school, including school buses, field trips, and other school events.

A Code of Conduct Committee—consisting of two members of the faculty, two parents, and a student representative—will be established by the principal. Suggested changes to the Code of Conduct should be submitted to this committee. If approved by the committee, the changes will be submitted to the principal for review.

**CHECK FOR UNDERSTANDING**

Why do you think these rules have been written? What is their purpose?

1. **General Rules**

a. Students are to walk at all times while in school.

b. Hats and backpacks brought to school are to be kept in the student's classroom. Once school starts, they are not to be worn in school.

c. Gum is not to be chewed while in school or on a school bus.

d. Parents of students who need to take medicine must contact the nurse. All medicines must be kept in their original bottles in the nurse's office. The nurse must receive a note explaining how the medicine is to be given.

e. Students are to be respectful toward the school staff and parents.

f. Students are to stand quietly at attention during the Pledge of Allegiance.

g. Students are expected to respect school property.

h. Students are expected to respect the property of others.

i. Problems are to be solved in a nonviolent manner. Fighting is not allowed.

*Students not following the general rules will receive detentions. Two violations will result in a call to the student's parents. Additional violations may result in a student being suspended.*

## 2. Lunchroom Behavior

Students have a right to eat in a safe and relaxed environment. All students are expected to:

a. walk into and leave the lunchroom in an orderly manner.
b. line up in the lunch line as directed by their teacher. There is to be no skipping or saving of places for other students.
c. clean the eating area before leaving the lunchroom.
d. wait quietly at their tables to be dismissed.
e. leave all food and drink in the lunchroom.
f. refrain from shouting or creating a disturbance of any kind.

*Students who do not follow these rules will not be allowed to eat in the lunchroom for a period of time determined by the severity of the violation.*

## 3. Bus Code of Conduct

Riding on a school bus is a privilege. The bus driver is in charge of all students on the bus. Any direction given by the driver is to be followed.

a. Students are to be courteous at all times while on the bus.
b. Students are not to open the windows without the permission of the school bus driver.
c. Students are to talk in a normal tone of voice at all times.
d. Students are to take assigned seats upon entering the bus.
e. Students are to remain seated until the bus reaches their stops.
f. Food or drinks are not to be consumed on the bus.
g. Students will be responsible for any damage done to the bus.

*Children who do not follow the Bus Code of Conduct will be punished. A detention will be given for the first offense. Additional offenses may cause the student to be removed from the bus.*

## 4. Student Dress

Students must dress properly when in school.

a. All clothing is to be neat, clean, and properly fitted.
b. Clothes with offensive pictures or language will not be allowed.
c. Footwear must be worn and securely fitted at all times.
d. Halter, tank, and tube tops will not be allowed.
e. Shorts are allowed only during warm weather.

*Students wearing unacceptable clothing will be sent home to change into appropriate clothing and may also receive a detention.* ∎

1. **Why did the auther most likely write this passage?**
   A. to describe the punishment for shouting
   B. to explain the rules of behavior
   C. to entertain with stories of student misbehavior
   D. to encourage students to get better grades

   *HINT: This question asks you to identify the central idea of the passage. Which answer best describes the passage?*

2. **Why should students not open the windows without the bus driver's permission?**
   A. to avoid being hurt on the bus
   B. to get more work done at school
   C. to allow more students to fit on the bus
   D. to help the bus driver move more quickly

   *HINT: This question asks you to think about information from the passage. If you are unsure of the answer, reread the Bus Code of Conduct section.*

3. **Who should first hear an idea for a new rule?**
   A. the principal
   B. teachers
   C. the committee
   D. students

   *HINT: This question asks you to recall a detail from the passage. If you are unsure of the answer, reread the introduction to the Code of Conduct.*

4. **How is this passage organized?**
   A. by listing types of rules
   B. by listing kinds of punishments
   C. by telling how often the rules are broken
   D. by telling how upset the principal is

   *HINT: This question asks you to recognize the way the text is organized. Look at the passage again. How did the author separate the information?*

**5. How would a student most likely first be punished for fighting on the bus?**

A. The student would be suspended.

B. The student's parents would receive a call at home.

C. The student would not be let on the bus.

D. The student would receive detention.

*HINT: This question asks you to draw a conclusion based on the passage. What did the passage say about punishment for misbehavior on the bus? If you are unsure of the answer, reread the Bus Code of Conduct section.*

**6. A student should read the code of conduct in order to**

A. see if he or she can think of another rule.

B. make sure he or she is following the rules.

C. know why his or her parents are angry.

D. check when his or her homework is due.

*HINT: This question asks you to think about the passage. Why do you think the students should read the Code of Conduct?*

**7. What does the word "privilege" mean as used in the "Bus Code of Conduct" section?**

A. listing

B. need

C. special right

D. serious problem

*HINT: This question asks you to identify the meaning of the word "privilege." Are there any clues to the word's meaning in the sentence?*

**8. Which of the following is a student allowed to wear according to the dress code?**

A. a hat

B. tank tops in the fall

C. shorts in the winter

D. a sweater

*HINT: This question asks you to recall a detail from the passage. If you are unsure of the answer, reread the Student Dress part of the passage.*

**FOR THE OPEN-ENDED QUESTION BELOW, REMEMBER TO:**
- Pay attention to what the question is asking you.
- Be sure to answer everything the question asks you.
- Fully explain what you mean by your answer.
- Use details from the story/passage.

9. A rip in Bob's assigned bus seat was found after the students got off at the school. The principal called Bob's father and told him he would have to pay for the damage. Bob's father replied that the damage was accidental, so he should not have to pay.

 • Explain who you believe is correct, the principal or Bob's father.

 Use information from the passage to support your response.

**FOR THE OPEN-ENDED QUESTION BELOW, REMEMBER TO:**
• Pay attention to what the question is asking you.
• Be sure to answer everything the question asks you.
• Fully explain what you mean by your answer.
• Use details from the story/passage.

10. Monique's classmates feel that the Code of Conduct is too strict. They have agreed to try to make changes to the code.
    • What process should they follow in order to make changes?
    Use information from the passage to support your response.

_____

_____

_____

_____

_____

_____

_____

_____

_____

_____

## YOU TRY IT

| DIRECTIONS INTRODUCTION | Read this story/passage and answer the questions that follow. Everyone has seen an ant. Almost all of these ants are harmless to animals and humans. Some ants, however, can be very dangerous. This passage talks about two of the most dangerous kinds of ants in the world. |
| --- | --- |

# The Dreaded Ant

Ants are found everywhere on earth except in Iceland, Greenland, and the Antarctic. There are thousands of species. Most of these ants are known only in the areas in which they are found.

One group of ants is known the world over and has even been the villain in several movies. They are the army ants, and they are among the fiercest predators on earth. They kill more animals and insects than all the big predators combined.

Actually, there are two types of army ants. The type that lives in South America are called "army ants." The type that lives in Africa and India are called "driver ants." While both are swarm raider ants, there are differences. The South American army ant has a stinger that is used to paralyze its prey. The African and Indian driver ant has large, sharp claws, used to injure its prey. Fortunately, only in rare cases have either type of ant killed a human.

The swarm of ants moves like a monstrous black tide about 20 yards wide. This is what strikes fear into most people caught in the path of army ants. Everything in the ants' path is killed. Insects do try to escape. However, if a few ants latch onto an insect as it is escaping, they will slow it down until the rest of the ants catch up. The swarm of ants will then cover and eat the insect.

> ✔ **CHECK FOR UNDERSTANDING**
>
> What traits do army ants have that explain how they got their name?

There have been cases where army ants and driver ants have attacked people. Cases involving the killing of people are rare, however. More often, ants will kill insects and sometimes even animals as large as pigs and cows.

Some parts of the world look forward to visits by army ants or driver ants. When these ants are seen coming toward a village, everyone leaves. The people will also take their animals with them. After the ants have passed through the village, all the houses will be clean. All vermin, snakes, and other insects in the town will be gone.

The success of both kinds of ants lies in their ability to work together. Small groups of scout ants go out looking for food. These ants leave a scent that larger groups of ants follow. Eventually, the entire colony will converge on the food source found by the scouts. It is only when the large group comes together that major damage is done to an area. These ants will eat over 100,000 animals and insects in a day.

An ant colony will often number over a million ants. Since there are so many ants, they are always looking for food. They are always on the move, usually traveling about 200 yards a day. At night, the ants will roll into a ball and build a nest for protection. The queen will then travel at night to a temporary camp. The next day, the ants will again move on.

After about 15 days, the army or driver ants will stop and set up a more permanent camp. The queen will stay in this camp or mound for about 20 days. She will lay up to 100,000 eggs. The worker ants will continue to forage for food in the general area. Each night they will return to the camp. After the eggs hatch, the colony again moves for the next 15 days, setting up temporary camps. ∎

**1. This passage is mostly about**

   A. why people fear army and driver ants.

   B. how army and driver ants live and hunt for food.

   C. how army and driver ants travel and set up camp.

   D. why the author likes army and driver ants.

*HINT: This question asks you to identify the central idea of the passage. Which answer best describes the passage?*

**2. What does the word "monstrous" mean in paragraph 4?**

   A. giant

   B. dark

   C. pleasing

   D. hairy

*HINT: This question asks you to identify the meaning of the word "monstrous." Are there any clues to the word's meaning in the sentence?*

**3. How are army ants different from driver ants?**

   A. Army ants are dangerous, and driver ants are not.

   B. Army ants travel, and driver ants stay in one place.

   C. Army ants are large, and driver ants are small.

   D. Army ants have stingers, and driver ants have claws.

*HINT: This question asks you to draw a conclusion based on the passage. How do army and driver ants differ? If you are unsure of the answer, reread the middle of the passage.*

**4. Why did the author most likely write this passage?**

   A. to teach readers how to avoid dangerous ants

   B. to entertain readers with funny stories about ants

   C. to persuade readers to learn about different types of ants

   D. to inform readers about army ants and driver ants

*HINT: This question asks you to recognize the way the text is organized. Look at the passage again. How did the author separate the information?*

**5. What do army ants and driver ants do each night?**

A. They break into small groups and look for food.

B. They travel about two hundred yards.

C. They roll into a ball and build a nest.

D. They protect the queen ant while she lays eggs.

*HINT: This question asks you to draw a conclusion based on the passage. What did the passage say about what army and driver ants do? If you are unsure of the answer, reread the middle of the passage.*

**6. The purpose of the seventh paragraph is to**

A. explain why readers should be afraid of ants.

B. tell the reader how the ants survive by working together.

C. tell the reader how to find a colony of army and driver ants.

D. explain why ants eat large animals.

*HINT: This question asks you to think about a particular paragraph within the passage. Reread paragraph 7 and ask yourself why the author wrote it.*

**7. Why do some people welcome army and driver ants into their towns?**

A. They want to give the queen ant a comfortable place to lay her eggs.

B. They want the ants to eats all of the vermin, snakes, and other insects in the town.

C. They want to gather all of the ants in one place so to get rid of them.

D. They want the ants to eat all of the animals in the town.

*HINT: This question asks you to draw a conclusion based on the passage. If you are unsure of the answer, reread the end of the passage.*

**FOR THE OPEN-ENDED QUESTION BELOW, REMEMBER TO:**
- Pay attention to what the question is asking you.
- Be sure to answer everything the question asks you.
- Fully explain what you mean by your answer.
- Use details from the story/passage.

8. **Army ants and driver ants travel and hunt in very interesting ways.**
   - **Briefly describe how army ants and driver ants work together to hunt for food.**
   - **Provide at least two details about how these ants hunt.**

   **Use information from the article to support your response.**

**FOR THE OPEN-ENDED QUESTION BELOW, REMEMBER TO:**
- Pay attention to what the question is asking you.
- Be sure to answer everything the question asks you.
- Fully explain what you mean by your answer.
- Use details from the story/passage.

9. Sometimes the names given to certain species seem to fit that species' behavior perfectly.
   - Why does the word "army" fit the kind of ants called "army ants"?

   Use information from the passage to support your response.

# CHAPTER 3

# Analyzing Text
## Text Organization and Extrapolation of Information

**RL.5.5; RI.5.5: RECOGNITION OF TEXT ORGANIZATION**

## YOU TRY IT

You have just finished reading an article in class. Your teacher asks you to explain why the passage was organized using steps. How do you answer?

- Do you look for the central idea of the story?
- Do you pull out a list of details to discuss?
- Do you study how the steps were organized and what purpose they serve?

The genre of the passage may help you understand the text organization. Think about what the story is trying to communicate. Why was it written? The way a passage is organized says a lot about what it is about.

## What is a genre?

A **genre** is a category used to define a type of writing.

There are several different types of genres. You are probably familiar with them already.

Some genres have sub-genres as well. A **sub-genre** can further explain what the story is about. Some sub-genres are science fiction, fantasy, and biography.

## What is a narrative?

Stories are **narratives**. They tell about one or more persons, an experience, or an event, usually in the order in which things happened.

Some of the many different kinds of stories are tall tales, adventure stories, legends, myths, folk tales, fairy tales, and mystery stories.

The body of writing called **fiction** is composed of made-up stories. The body of writing called **nonfiction** is composed of true or factual stories.

Sometimes, like in historical fiction, fiction and nonfiction overlap. An author may use known historical facts as the setting and the background for a story about individual characters who have been made up.

## What is an everyday text?

An author writes an **everyday text** either to tell the readers how to do something or to give them information that will be useful for their daily lives.

Depending on the topic or theme, everyday texts usually have directions or steps. In order to understand an everyday text, you have to look at the way it is organized. If it has steps, the steps are usually numbered (Step 1, Step 2…).

There may be pictures along with the steps to illustrate exactly how to do something.

If there are pictures, like in the recipe below, look carefully at each picture and pay attention to how the picture goes along with the text you are reading. You may have to answer questions about it.

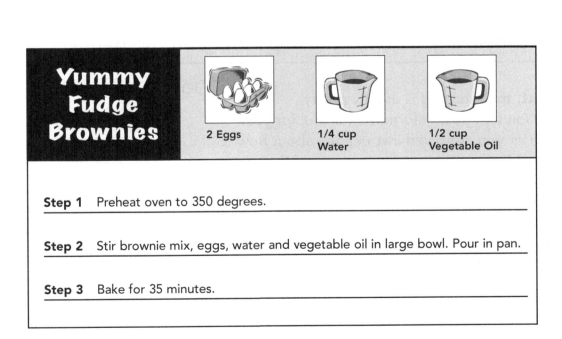

**Yummy Fudge Brownies**

2 Eggs | 1/4 cup Water | 1/2 cup Vegetable Oil

**Step 1** Preheat oven to 350 degrees.

**Step 2** Stir brownie mix, eggs, water and vegetable oil in large bowl. Pour in pan.

**Step 3** Bake for 35 minutes.

## Does the genre help me to determine the meaning?

Before you read a passage, are you able to identify its genre? Can you tell just by looking at the title what kind of writing it might be?

If you can, you will be a step ahead as you work your way toward completely understanding what you read.

What are some questions you can ask yourself about a passage—before, while, or after you read it—that will let you know which genre it is? Here are a few to get you started:

- What is the central idea of the story?
- How is the text organized?
- What is the style of the text?

## Would the meaning be different depending on the genre?

In **everyday text,** the meaning is usually pretty straightforward. You are given information useful for your everyday life and/or you are given instructions about how to make or do something.

In **narrative writing**, however, there can be layers of meaning. Sometimes authors tell you everything you need to know in a story. They use exact words. This information is called **explicit meaning**. But, many times an author does not tell you everything you need to know. Some things about a story are not directly stated. This information is the **implicit meaning**. When there is implicit meaning in a story, you must figure out the deeper meaning for yourself. The author does not come out and tell you the meaning.

## RL.5.5; RI.5.5: RECOGNITION OF TEXT ORGANIZATION

Each passage has three important parts. No matter how short or long a passage is, it has to have a **beginning**, a **middle**, and an **end**.

### BEGINNING

- The beginning of the passage is the first paragraph, paragraphs, or even pages, depending on the length of the passage.

- In the beginning of any passage, you will be introduced to the setting and the characters.

**SETTING:** the time and place, where the story takes place

**CHARACTERS:** the people in the passage

### MIDDLE

- The middle of the passage is the next paragraph, paragraphs, or pages, depending on the length of the passage. During this part of the passage, you will learn about the plot.

**PLOT:** this is basically what the passage is about, the path the passage takes, and what happens

### END

- The end of the passage is the final paragraph, paragraphs, or pages, depending on the length of the passage. The end of the passage contains the conclusion.

**CONCLUSION:** this is how the passage wraps up the plot; it explains how everything turns out

## LET'S TRY IT TOGETHER

**DIRECTIONS**   Read the story/passage and together we will discuss the questions.

# Danica's Hero

As Danica walked out her front door and onto the sidewalk, she took a deep breath in. She could smell the cherry blossoms from down the street. The smell reminded her why spring is her favorite time of year. A lot of people would probably say spring is their favorite time of year, but Danica thinks there is something special about springtime in Washington, D.C.

It's clear that she's not the only one who thinks this is the best time of year to be in the nation's capital; it is one of the busiest times for tourists. Danica made her way through the busy streets, being careful not to walk in front of any of the crowds of people admiring and taking pictures of the monuments.

She looked up at the Washington memorial in the distance. *I am so lucky I live in such a fascinating place,* she thought to herself.

The crowd next to her shifted. Before she could even realize it, Danica ended up in the busy roadway.

"Look out!" she heard someone yell.

She looked to her right and saw several cars headed in her direction. She began to panic.

Suddenly, she felt two large hands grab her by the waist.  The next thing she knew she was on the grass. She looked up and saw a man, dressed as a soldier. "What happened?" she asked.

"You fell out into the street," said the soldier. "Are you okay?"

Danica looked past the soldier and saw the busy street over his shoulder; cars were whizzing by, one after another. She felt fine, just scared. It had been a very close call.

"I'm… I'm okay," Danica said, still in disbelief. She stood up and wiped off her jeans. She saw the road again.

"Wow. You saved my life," Danica said, staring up at the soldier. "You're my hero."

The soldier smiled. "Just doing my job." ∎

## What were the three parts of this story?

**Beginning**
Danica leaves her house and walks down the street.

▼

**Middle**
Danica gets pushed into the street by a crowd.

▼

**End**
Danica is saved by a soldier, her "hero."

**Explore CCSS/PARCC Grade 5 Reading** © 2014 Queue, Inc. All rights reserved.

**79**

## What genre is this story?

**Is this an example of everyday text?**
No, this is not an example of everyday text. How do we know? We have learned that in everyday text, the author is trying to inform the reader about something. That is not the case in this story. Also, there are no steps or numbered points in this story.

**Is this an example of narrative text?**
Yes, this story is an example of narrative text. How do we know? This story is about Danica taking a walk and getting rescued. It tells what happens in an organized way.

## What is the author *really* trying to say?

**What is the explicit meaning of this story?**
We already know that what the words tell us is the **explicit meaning**.

In this story, the words tell us that Danica is saved by a soldier. So the story is saying that soldiers are heroes.

**What is the implicit meaning of this story?**
The **implicit meaning** in a story is not expressed in words. You can get this meaning by thinking about what the story is telling you. Then ask yourself what the larger meaning might be.

In this story, the implicit meaning is to be careful when you're walking and to watch where you are going.

## YOU TRY IT

| | |
|---|---|
| **DIRECTIONS** **INTRODUCTION** | Read this passage and answer the questions that follow. Francis Chichester circumnavigated the globe around Cape Horn in his yacht, *Gipsy Moth IV*. Circumnavigation means "passing two points that are exactly opposite each other on the surface of the earth." Let's read Chichester's story and find out how he did it. |

# Gipsy Moth IV

Imagine sailing alone around the world in a ship just 54 feet long. Only someone with great skill, determination, and courage would try it. One man, Francis Chichester, did it at the age of 65. His voyage would cover about 30,000 miles. Two other men had made similar voyages, but it took one man three years and the other seven years. The fastest round-the-world trip had taken one year and nine days and was only 20,000 miles long. Francis wanted to make the longer trip, and he wanted to do it in record time. To make his historic trip, Francis had a fast boat built. He named it *Gipsy Moth IV*.

**1**

Along with his wife and son, Francis worked for months planning for the trip. There were maps and charts of ocean currents and wind currents to gather. Records of lighthouses and signals for dangerous reefs and shoals were needed. Also, knowing the weather around the world for each month was very important.

For most of the trip, land would be out of sight. Therefore, Francis had to know how to use the sun and the stars to tell where he was. This method took a lot of math. The results of these calculations are called "dead reckoning."

Francis planned on making only one stop – at Sydney, Australia. The city is about 14,000 miles from England. The plan required him to have lots of canned and fresh food, medicines, tools, and replacement parts. Lists were made of these hundreds of items, along with notations of where each was stored.

Weeks before the start of the trip, Francis fell and injured his leg. By the time he sailed, it still had not healed. The pain kept him awake and made walking and balancing a problem. This injury bothered him throughout the trip.

Collisions with other boats became the first danger Francis faced. All but fishing boats must give way to sailboats. However, large ships might not see a small yacht. That made sailing near shipping lanes very dangerous. So, most of this trip took place in areas where ships don't usually travel. Due to these dangerous conditions, whenever Francis tried to sleep, he would hang two red lights on the mast. This signaled "Out of Control" and told other ships that, at this particular time, no one was steering the boat. Even so, on two occasions, he almost had accidents.

Sailing alone is a lot of work. Winds and weather change often during a 24-hour period. Different sails are needed for different conditions. Many times, night and day, Francis had to change sails or correct his course. Water leaked into the boat in many places. Waves washed over the deck, sending gallons of water down into the cabin. Francis spent hours fixing as many leaks as he could. Mold, mildew, and wet clothes and gear became a constant problem. Almost all of 16 dozen eggs had to be thrown overboard. Moldy bread had to be rebaked. Some cheeses and fruits became food for the circling birds.

**CHECK FOR UNDERSTANDING**

Why would Francis need to create a detailed plan before his trip? Why were all the things he gathered important?

**8** In the midst of all that ocean water, getting fresh water was a problem. Francis rigged up a pipe to catch rainwater from the sails. Salt on the sails, however, made for salty water, which he had to use for washing clothes, bathing, cooking, and even drinking. Finally, rain came and filled his water tanks with fresh water.

Eighty days into the trip—more than 1,700 miles from Sydney—the steering oar broke. It couldn't be fixed. Instead of reaching Sydney in 20 days, it looked like it might take 50 or 55. He thought he would have to find a closer port. The trip seemed over. After many tries, he found a way to get some speed.

Francis wouldn't make it to Sydney in the planned 100 days. He did make it in 107 days, having sailed 14,100 miles. After two sleepless nights, he arrived 40 pounds lighter, with a bad leg. He received a hero's welcome. Best of all, his relieved wife and son were there to greet him.

**11** After seven weeks and much work, the ship was ready for the trip home. Many people thought Francis was foolish to go on. Even for very large ships, rounding Cape Horn, the southernmost tip of South America, was very dangerous. But Francis couldn't bring himself to quit. He did do something foolish, however, that almost cost him his life.

Francis insisted on leaving Sydney even though Tropic Cyclone Diana was northeast of the city. He thought he could avoid the worst of the storm. Caught in it the next night, the *Gipsy Moth IV* capsized. She didn't roll over, however, and managed to right herself. Everything in lockers on the right side ended up on the floor. Wet vitamin tablets stuck to the roof. Broken glass wound up in strange places. Butter was everywhere. Clothes, hangers, and the first aid kit were in the sink. The bunks had collapsed. On deck, many things were misplaced or broken. Part of the cockpit above Francis's bunk was torn away. He was lucky, though. He had survived. He was so tired that he lay down on his soaking wet bunk and fell asleep. The cleanup and repairs would have to wait.

**12**

The next morning, Francis called Sydney on his radio telephone to tell them what had happened, but he refused help. Instead, he made a list of 71 things he had to do before reaching Cape Horn.

Cape Horn can be a ship's nightmare. It is the tip of an island where the Atlantic and Pacific Oceans meet. Fierce winds come around the Atlas Mountains and through Drake Strait.

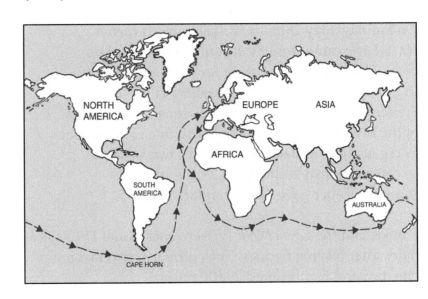

The depth of the ocean bottom creates waves easily 60 feet high. Some reach 100 feet high or more. As expected, this was a rough part of the trip. On seeing the Horn, Francis recorded that its 1,400-foot cliff looked "like a black ice-cream cone."

Two unexpected things happened there. A British warship and a plane both appeared. Hearing Francis's radio message to Buenos Aires, Argentina, they came to see if he was all right. Even after he rounded the Horn, weather and winds were fierce. They kept driving the ship either in circles or backwards. On April 11th, Francis crossed his outward-bound track. At that point, he had circumnavigated the globe. It had taken 190 days and 13 hours, including his time in port. England, however, was still more than 5,000 miles away.

Before long, *Gipsy Moth IV* entered the doldrums of the South Atlantic. Days went by with little forward progress. Francis nursed a painfully swollen and infected elbow, the result of a fall. To get any rest or to perform tasks, he had to take painkillers. Adding to his discomfort were his injured leg and a bruised ankle and ribs from an earlier fall.

*British aircraft carrier HMS Eagle saluting the* **Gipsy Moth IV**

Eventually, the winds and seas turned more favorable. Yet, when Francis was almost within sight of Plymouth Harbor in Massachusetts, the sea continued to play tricks. Television ships had gathered to photograph and welcome the ship home.

On Sunday, May 28th, the British aircraft carrier *HMS Eagle* came close by. Its entire crew lined the deck. They gave three cheers for the *Gipsy Moth IV*. In the book he wrote to tell the story of this trip, Francis said, "It must surely be unique in the history of the British Navy for a warship with a complement as big as the population of a small town to salute so ceremoniously a ship with a crew of one!"[1] A minesweeper gave him a similar salute.

**Gipsy Moth IV** *coming into port.*

Francis and the *Gipsy Moth IV* were back home 119 days and 15,517 miles after leaving Sydney. The entire trip had taken nine months and one day, and had covered 29,630 miles.

*Sir Francis Chichester*

In honor of his efforts, Queen Elizabeth II knighted Francis. All of London honored this courageous sailor who had set seven sailing records as he made this *incredible* solo journey. ∎

[1] *Quotes are from Chichester, Francis, Gipsy Moth, New York: Coward-McCann, Inc., 1967 (First American Edition—1968). This book is based on the logs Chichester kept during his voyage. It is written in terms that would be best understood by someone very familiar with sailboat design, the sailing of these boats, preparations needed for long ocean trips, and ocean navigation.*

*Queen Elizabeth II knighting Sir Francis Chichester*

1. **Who helped Francis Chichester to plan his trip around the world?**
   A. people who had made the trip
   B. his family
   C. Queen Elizabeth II
   D. the navy

*HINT: This question asks you to think about information from the passage. If you are unsure of the answer, reread the beginning of the passage.*

2. **Why were the sun and stars important to Francis Chichester during his trip?**
   A. They provided energy for the boat.
   B. They made him feel close to home.
   C. They helped him learn to do math.
   D. They helped him know his location.

*HINT: This question asks you to make a judgment based on the passage. How do you think the stars and sun could have been used by Francis?*

3. **What did it mean when Francis Chichester hung two red lights from his mast?**
   A. He was very ill.
   B. He was sleeping.
   C. He needed help.
   D. He had given up.

*HINT: This question asks you to recall a detail from the passage. If you are unsure of the answer, skim the passage. You should look for a mention of two red lights.*

4. **What lesson does this article teach?**
   A. Even when goals seem impossible, you should work hard to meet them.
   B. When you are lost at sea, you should stay as calm as you can.
   C. Aircraft carriers do not carry as many passengers as most people think.
   D. Sailing around the world is safer than flying around the world.

*HINT: This question asks you to identify the theme of the passage. What did you think after you completed reading the passage? What do you think the author was trying to say?*

5. **The purpose of the first sentence of this article is to**
   A. introduce the main person in the article.
   B. give an idea of what the trip might be like.
   C. explain how long Francis Chichester had been sailing.
   D. explain why Francis Chichester decided to make his trip.

*HINT: This question asks you to think about a particular part of the passage. Reread the first sentence and ask yourself why the author wrote it.*

6. **Why did Francis Chichester sail where *most* ships did not travel?**
   A. He wanted to be different.
   B. He did not like being around others.
   C. He did not want boats to hit him.
   D. He wanted to find new land.

*HINT: This question asks you to think about information from the passage. If you are unsure of the answer, reread the middle of the passage.*

7. **Why does the author describe the actions of Francis Chichester as "foolish" in the eleventh paragraph?**
   A. Francis Chichester wanted to sail around the world in record time.
   B. Francis Chichester decided to leave Australia during a bad storm.
   C. Francis Chichester would sail almost 30,000 miles during his trip.
   D. Francis Chichester decided to sail alone on his trip around the world.

*HINT: This question asks you to think about a particular paragraph within the passage. Reread paragraph 11 and ask yourself why the author might say that what Francis Chichester did was foolish.*

8. **What does the word "determination" mean in the first paragraph?**
   A. family
   B. power of body
   C. wealth
   D. strength of mind

*HINT: This question asks you to identify the meaning of the word "determination." Are there any clues to the word's meaning in the sentence?*

**9. What was Francis Chichester's main problem as he sailed through the South Atlantic?**
A. He had many injuries.
B. He had to take medicine.
C. He had no drinking water.
D. He had no food left.

*HINT: his question asks you to draw a conclusion based on the passage. Based on what you have read, what was Chichester's main difficulty?*

**10. What does the word "midst" mean in the eighth paragraph of the article?**
A. safety
B. heat
C. middle
D. transfer

*HINT: This question asks you to identify the meaning of the word "midst." Are there any clues to the word's meaning in the sentence?*

**11. What does the word "wound" mean in paragraph 12?**
A. ended up
B. wrapped up
C. an open sore
D. an old rope

*HINT: This question asks you to identify the meaning of the word "wound." Are there any clues to the word's meaning in the sentence?*

**12. Francis Chichester said,**
"It must surely be unique in the history of the British Navy for a warship with a complement as big as the population of a small town to salute so ceremoniously a ship with a crew of one!"
**This means that he felt**
A. drained.
B. confused.
C. honored.
D. nervous.

*HINT: This question asks you to determine what someone meant. Based on what you have read, what might Chichester have meant?*

**FOR THE OPEN-ENDED QUESTION BELOW, REMEMBER TO:**
• Pay attention to what the question is asking you.
• Be sure to answer everything the question asks you.
• Fully explain what you mean by your answer.
• Use details from the story/passage.

13. Francis Chichester must have had some pleasant sunny days that were trouble-free.
    • **Explain why the author most likely did not tell about these kinds of days in the story. Use information from the article to support your response.**

**FOR THE OPEN-ENDED QUESTION BELOW, REMEMBER TO:**
• Pay attention to what the question is asking you.
• Be sure to answer everything the question asks you.
• Fully explain what you mean by your answer.
• Use details from the story/passage.

14. The other two men who had made similar round-the-world trips took three years and seven years to complete them, respectively.
    • **Why might it have taken them so long when Francis Chichester did it in nine months and one day?**
    • **Give at least four reasons in your response.**
    **Use information from the article to support your response.**

## YOU TRY IT

**DIRECTIONS**   Read the passage below and answer the questions that follow.

# Friends Aren't Always Fair

When Ellen entered the house, she closed the front door firmly. You might even say she slammed it shut. Her mother was in the kitchen, waiting for Ellen to come in and announce that she was starving. Growing young men and women seem to always be hungry! Mrs. Thomas thought.

Mrs. Thomas waited before finally calling out, "Ellen, where are you?"

There was no answer. Mrs. Thomas wondered if something was wrong. Then, noticing Ellen's book bag lying unopened on the hall table, she walked slowly toward the front door. Ellen was nowhere in sight. Mrs. Thomas called up the stairs, but again, there was no answer.

Sensing that something was definitely amiss, Mrs. Thomas quickly climbed the stairs. Although Ellen's bedroom door was closed, her mother could hear her moving about inside. Mrs. Thomas tapped on the door, "Ellen, it's me. Can I... talk to you?"

Ellen mumbled something that her mother couldn't quite understand. Mrs. Thomas turned the knob and pushed the door open. There was Ellen standing in the middle of the room with red eyes and nose. All her stuffed animals were in disarray on her bed. Even her small animal collection that normally decorated the

**✔ CHECK FOR UNDERSTANDING**

What do you think has upset Ellen? Why would she be acting the way she is?

shelves was thrown around and her dolls were in a pile on the bed. Obviously, something had upset Ellen and her mother wasn't sure what it was.

Before she could speak, however, Ellen said, "Do we have a big box somewhere? I want to get rid of these things. Maybe some little kid would want them."

Mrs. Thomas was surprised, but managed not to show it. This was not like Ellen. She had loved collecting these stuffed animals and had always taken very good care of them. She had even given them names. Whatever could have happened to make her think of giving them away?

Mrs. Thomas said, "I think we have a box in the basement. Why don't you have a glass of milk and something to eat? Then I'll help you look for a box."

"You go ahead, Mom. I'll be down in a minute."

As her mother slowly descended the stairs, she heard the water running in the bathroom. Ellen was patting cold water on her eyes and washing her face.

In a few minutes, she walked into the kitchen. Her mother said, "I think I'll just sit and have a cup of tea while you are eating." She started chatting about this and that, but Ellen just sat there with a long, sad face, saying nothing. Finally, her mother inquired, "Will Danesha or some of your other friends be coming over today?"

"No, and I'm never going to speak to Danesha again. That goes for Tina and Nancy, too!" Ellen declared crossly.

"Did something happen between you and your friends? Does it have anything to do with you giving your things away?"

Ellen swallowed hard and tried to blink back tears. "I thought Danesha was my friend. Yesterday, I took her upstairs and showed her my collection of stuffed animals. She asked if I ever talked to them. I said that I did sometimes and that I say good night to them before I go to sleep."

"Well, there's nothing wrong with that. I talk to the cat when I'm alone here in the house. Your dad talks to the TV. He even talks to his tools when he's making something. We all talk to things sometimes," her mother assured her.

**16** "I know, but it just isn't fair. Danesha was laughing at school when she was telling everyone about my stuffed animals and how I talk to them. She said I was a baby like her little brother. He plays with toys and talks to them like I do. But forget it. I'll give all of my animals away and then she can't say that I'm a baby."

"Ellen, will you feel any better if you give your animals away?"

Ellen was about to say yes, but she hesitated. "No, not really. I'll miss them. So many came from Gram and you as presents."

"Then why give them away? You know you're not a baby. Well, of course," she mused, "your dad does call you Baby, but that's different."

"Oh, Mom, I know that," Ellen said, breaking into a smile.

"Come on, I'll help you put your animals back where they belong," she said, hugging her daughter.

"Remember, friends may hurt our feelings, but real friends accept us for who we are and usually find a way of making up." ■

1. **Why was Ellen angry with Danesha?**
   A. Danesha asked if Ellen ever talked to her collection of stuffed animals.
   B. Danesha told Ellen to get rid of her collection of stuffed animals.
   C. Danesha laughed at Ellen and called her a baby.
   D. Danesha played with toys and talked to them.

*HINT: This question asks you to recall a detail from the passage. If you are unsure of the answer, reread the middle of the passage. You should look for a reason why Ellen would be angry.*

2. **Read the following sentence from the passage.**
   "She started *chatting* about this and that, but Ellen just sat there with a long, sad face, saying nothing."
   **What does the word "chatting" mean in the passage?**
   A. talking
   B. listening
   C. singing
   D. thinking

*HINT: This question asks you to identify the meaning of the word "chatting." Are there any clues in the sentence?*

3. **"Sensing that something was definitely amiss" means that Mrs. Thomas**
   A. wasn't concerned with what Ellen was upset about.
   B. was angry that Ellen's book bag was on the hall table.
   C. couldn't find Ellen anywhere in the house.
   D. knew Ellen was upset about something.

*HINT: This question asks you to predict what the author meant. What does that phrase mean within the passage?*

4. **Where did the story take place?**
   A. at Danesha's house
   B. at Ellen's house
   C. in the school cafeteria
   D. in the school hallway

*HINT: This question asks you to recognize the setting of the passage. If you unsure of the answer, skim the passage, looking for clues about the story location.*

**5. Ellen would miss her collection of stuffed animals because**

    A.  many came from her Gram and mother as presents.

    B.  she was hoping to give them to her baby brother.

    C.  she and Danesha liked to play with them after school.

    D.  many came from Danesha, Tina, and Nancy as presents.

*HINT: This question asks you to draw a conclusion based on the passage. Based on what you have read, why was the animal collection significant to Ellen?*

**6. What is the purpose of paragraph 16?**

    A.  to tell readers that Mrs. Thomas was a very caring mother.

    B.  to describe to readers the mess Ellen had made in her bedroom.

    C.  to explain to readers why Ellen was angry with Danesha.

    D.  to inform readers about where Ellen had gotten her collection of animals.

*HINT: This question asks you to think about the way the text is organized. Why do you think the author wrote this paragraph?*

**FOR THE OPEN-ENDED QUESTION BELOW, REMEMBER TO:**
- Pay attention to what the question is asking you.
- Be sure to answer everything the question asks you.
- Fully explain what you mean by your answer.
- Use details from the story/passage.

7. While Mrs. Thomas is worried about Ellen's happiness, she doesn't react very emotionally about Ellen's disagreement with Danesha.
   - How does her attitude about the situation in the story reflect this?
   - What does her mother most likely understand about friendships between young girls?

   Use information from the passage to support your response.

## YOU TRY IT

| | |
|---|---|
| **DIRECTIONS** | Read this story/passage and answer the questions that follow. |
| **INTRODUCTION** | On July 25, 1956, a ship called the *Stockholm* collided with another ship, the *Andrea Doria*. This event became one of the greatest sea rescues in history. Read this passage to find out why this was considered to have been such a great sea rescue. |

**VOCABULARY TERMS YOU SHOULD KNOW**

| | |
|---|---|
| **foghorn** | a horn warning ships about fog |
| **list** | to lean over to one side |
| **liner** | a ship or aircraft that carries people on a regular line, or route |
| **port side** | the left-hand side of the boat |
| **radar** | system for detecting the presence of objects by reflecting radio waves |
| **starboard** | the right-hand side of the boat |
| **s.o.s.** | morse code message of distress meaning "Save Our Ship" |

# A Great Sea Rescue

The *Andrea Doria* was the most modern liner of its day. The ship had every comfort available at the time. It had all of the newest safety equipment, including watertight doors to stop it from sinking. It also had the latest radio and radar equipment. The ship carried 16 lifeboats that could collectively hold over 2,000 people. Even with all this safety equipment, the ship sank in just 11 hours.

On July 25th, the *Andrea Doria* was nearing New York Harbor amidst a heavy fog. It was ending its 51st round trip across the Atlantic. By 9:00 p.m., the fog was so thick that hardly anything could be seen. Captain Calamai was using radar to steer the ship. The foghorn was being blown on a regular basis.

**3** The *Andrea Doria*, however, was not alone on the sea that night. The *Stockholm*, a Swedish ship, was nearby. At about 10:00 p.m., the *Andrea Doria* spotted the *Stockholm* on its radar. Captain Calamai thought the *Stockholm* would change course, but it did not. Both ships continued to sail towards each other. Suddenly, the *Stockholm* appeared from out of the fog. It was on a collision course with the *Andrea Doria*. Both ships tried to turn, but it was too late. At 11:10 p.m., the *Stockholm* plowed into the side of the *Andrea Doria*.

The crew of the *Stockholm* immediately reversed its engines. As it pulled away, it left a 40-foot-wide hole in the side of the *Andrea Doria*. Seawater poured in and the ship began to list slightly to starboard. It continued to lean to the right for quite some time.

The watertight doors could not keep the seawater out. The hole was too large. In less than an hour, the captain knew his ship was doomed. He gave the order to abandon the ship. The radio operator sent out an SOS. Ships in the area started steaming toward the *Andrea Doria* to offer help.

Many of the lifeboats on-board the *Andrea Doria* couldn't be used. Those on the port side were wedged against the ship and were therefore useless. The boats were so heavy that the crew could not move them. Lifeboats on the starboard side were also a problem. Because of the dangerous way in which the ship was leaning, these lifeboats were hanging far away from the boat. No one could step into these boats before they were lowered into the ocean. Then, the crew could rig ropes for people to slide down into the waiting lifeboats. More than an hour passed before the first lifeboats left the ship. These boats had more crew members on them than passengers.

*The* Stockholm *after colliding with the* Andrea Doria

Soon after it pulled away, the *Stockholm* began offering its lifeboats to rescue people in the water. Lifeboats from other ships also joined in the rescue. It was hours later before most of the passengers were off the *Andrea Doria*. Many first- and cabin-class passengers had to wait three hours before boarding a lifeboat. It took even longer for passengers on the lower decks. They had to wade through seawater to reach the boat decks. Once there, they had to wait for hours for an open lifeboat. Many people decided not to wait. They jumped into the water and swam to the lifeboats.

**✔ CHECK FOR UNDERSTANDING**

How did the collision happen? Do you think it could have been prevented?

What is amazing is that so few people lost their lives in this disaster. A total of 51 people died as a result of the collision. The *Stockholm* lost five men. The other 46 deaths were from the *Andrea Doria*. All these people died as a direct result of the collision. The rescue boats were able to save more than 1,600 people.

The sinking of the *Andrea Doria* was the first sea disaster to be recorded by the media. TV and radio crews came to the disaster site. This was the first time the world watched and listened as people were being rescued at sea. Audiences experienced the pain and suffering of the people in the water. They also watched and listened as the *Andrea Doria* sank. In the end, people rejoiced at the low loss of life. Never before had so many people seen or heard a real sea disaster.

After the sinking of the *Andrea Doria*, there was a Court of Inquiry. Officers from both ships testified. They explained what had happened on board their ships. The court said that the *Andrea Doria* should have followed the ocean "Rule of the Road." This rule says that when two ships are sailing towards each other, each should turn right. Following this rule would have caused them to turn away from each other. The court's final decision blamed the heavy fog for the accident. The *Stockholm* was able to steam back into New York Harbor. After repairs, it continued to sail for many years. ∎

*The* Andrea Doria *sinking.*

**1. What is this article mostly about?**

    A. how the public reacted to the sinking of the *Andrea Doria*

    B. how the crew and passengers acted when the *Andrea Doria* was hit

    C. why the media showed great interest in the *Andrea Doria*

    D. why the authorities sued and punished the crew of the *Andrea Doria*

*HINT: This question asks you to identify the central idea of the passage. Think about what you have read. What do you think the author was trying to tell you about?*

**2. Why couldn't people use the lifeboats on the *Andrea Doria*?**

    A. The crew refused to let them on the lifeboats.

    B. The lifeboats were filled with seawater.

    C. Some boats were damaged, while others could not float.

    D. Some boats were stuck, while others could not be easily reached.

*HINT: This question asks you to think about information from the passage. If you are unsure of the answer, skim the passage looking for a mention of lifeboats.*

**3. What does the word "collision" mean as it was used in paragraph 3?**

    A. crash

    B. warrior

    C. thankful

    D. property

*HINT: This question asks you to identify the meaning of the word "collision." Are there any clues to the word's meaning in the paragraph?*

**4. Although *"A Great Sea Rescue"* is about the *Andrea Doria* disaster, it would be useful background reading for an oral report on**

    A. the lives of the people who built the Stockholm.

    B. how stories change over a long period of time.

    C. the history of how the media deals with disaster.

    D. how to handle a group of people who are upset.

*HINT: This question asks you to think about the passage. What is the explicit meaning of the text? If you are unsure of the answer, skim the passage.*

**5. How did ships in the area know they should come to help the *Andrea Doria*?**

   A.  The other ships in the area heard the sounds of the crash.

   B.  The media alerted all people in the area of the disaster.

   C.  A crewmember of the *Andrea Doria* radioed for help.

   D.  A crewmember of the Stockholm spread the message.

*HINT: This question asks you to think about information from the passage. If you are unsure of the answer, reread the middle of the passage.*

**FOR THE OPEN-ENDED QUESTION BELOW, REMEMBER TO:**
• Pay attention to what the question is asking you.
• Be sure to answer everything the question asks you.
• Fully explain what you mean by your answer.
• Use details from the story/passage.

6. The cause of this accident at sea was found to be the fog, but the entire unfortunate event could probably have been prevented.
  • Explain what both ships could have done to avoid colliding with one another.
  • Include details about what Captain Calamai was doing before the accident to keep his ship safe.
  Use information from the passage to support your response.

## YOU TRY IT

**DIRECTIONS** Read the passage below and answer the questions that follow.

# Building a Viking Longboat

The Vikings were excellent shipbuilders. Their longboats were superior to all other ships of their time. They made it possible for the Vikings to travel great distances. Longboats could withstand the major storms of the Atlantic Ocean. Even the largest of these ships was light enough to be carried or rolled over land.

A Viking longboat was long and slender with a high bow and stern. It had holes for oars, which were used when the boat was close to shore. The Vikings were the first sailors to use sails to move their ships. The sail, used when the ship was in open water, allowed it to travel faster than other ships of its time. They were also the first shipbuilders to use a keel on their ships. This helped reduce the roll of the ship when in open water. The keel also improved the steering of the longboat.

**Stages of Building a Viking Longboat**
Viking longboats were built from the bottom up. First, the keel and stems were made (*Figure 1*). Keels were always made from oak. The length of the keel determined the size and curved shape of the front and back stem.

The sides of the longboat were made of overlapping planks called strakes. Next, these planks were added

**✔ CHECK FOR UNDERSTANDING**

What features of the longboats made them superior to other ships of their time?

to the ship from the bottom up until the sides were at the proper height (*Figure 1*). Each plank overlapped the one below it. The Vikings split large oak trees to make these strakes. Freshly cut trees were used because it was easier to work with green wood. The strakes were shaped as they were put onto the keel and stems.

Iron rivets were used to hold the planks together and strips of smoked rope were stuffed between the planks where they overlapped to make a watertight seal. Using rope between the planks also allowed the ship to flex in rough seas and helped to prevent it from breaking up during storms.

Rowing holes were cut into the side of the longboat at a height suitable for a man to row when seated. The first longboats had their oars fastened on the top of the rails of the ship. As the Vikings began exploring further from land, they made longboats with higher sides. This reduced the chance of water flowing into the boats as they rolled on the ocean. The higher sides required that rowing holes be cut into the sides of the hull so that rowers could still remain seated while rowing (*Figure 2*).

To keep the sides of the ship watertight, wooden disks were hinged to oar holes and placed in the row holes when the oars were not used.

Frames were added after the bottom and sides were completed, strengthening

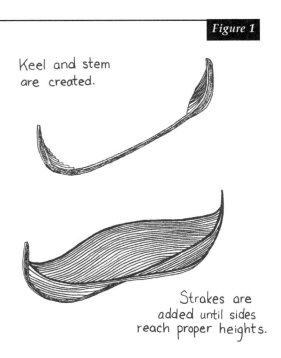

**Figure 1**

Keel and stem are created.

Strakes are added until sides reach proper heights.

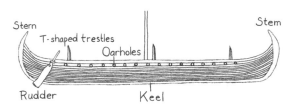

**Figure 2**

Stern

T-shaped trestles

Oarholes

Stem

Rudder

Keel

the hull of the longboat (*Figure 3*). The crossbeams made the hull stronger and were added after the frames (*Figure 3*). The rowers sat on the crossbeams while rowing.

As the sides of the longboat were made to be higher, portable decks were built on the crossbeams. When it was necessary to row, the deck could be removed and the Viking soldiers could sit on the crossbeams.

Once the crossbeams were installed, the mast was added. The mast was inserted into a socket in the keelson, a large block of wood above the keel.

After the mast was attached, a floor was built in the bottom of the boat and additional supports were attached to both the mast and the floor. These helped to secure the mast more firmly (*Figure 4*).

**12** A large steering oar was then attached to the right side of the boat near the stern. A fierce-looking figurehead was carved and put on the bow of the longboat (*Figure 5*). The Vikings believed that the figurehead would help to keep sea monsters from sinking the ship when it was far from shore. ■

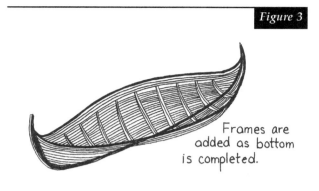

Figure 3

Frames are added as bottom is completed.

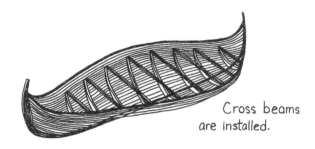

Cross beams are installed.

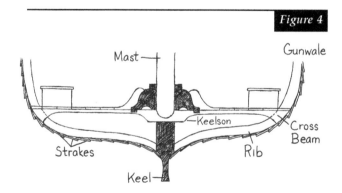

Figure 4

Mast — Gunwale

Keelson

Cross Beam

Strakes

Rib

Keel —

Figure 5

**1. What is the first thing you should do when making a Viking longboat?**

A. measure the oars

B. build the stems

C. sew the sail together

D. make the keels

HINT: *This question asks you to think about the way the text is organized. What was the first step of building a longboat?*

**3. Why did the Vikings use freshly cut trees to make strakes?**

A. New wood lasted the longest.

B. Strakes needed to still be wet.

C. New wood was easiest to work with.

D. They had a hard time finding trees.

HINT: *This question asks you to recall a detail from the passage. If you are unsure of the answer, reread the first stage of building a longboat.*

**2. Read the following sentence from the passage.**

"The sides of the longboat were made of overlapping planks called *strakes*."

**What does the word "strakes" mean?**

A. things that stick out of the ground

B. wood the Vikings used

C. planks on the side of a longboat

D. the masts that held the sails

HINT: *This question asks you to identify the meaning of the word "strakes." Are there any clues to the word's meaning in the sentence?*

**4. What allowed the sides of the longboats to flex when in rough seas?**

A. The rope between the planks moved in rough water.

B. The planks were thin enough to bend in rough water.

C. The iron rivets allowed the planks to move freely.

D. The crossbeams that held the ship together were rubber.

HINT: *This question asks you to think about information from the passage. If you are unsure of the answer, reread the stages of building the longboat.*

**5. How did the figurehead on the boat help the Vikings?**
   A. It was used to steer the ship during storms.
   B. It made them feel safe from monsters.
   C. It showed them which way to go.
   D. It allowed the ship to float.

*HINT: This question asks you to draw a conclusion based on the passage. If you are unsure of the answer, reread the end of the passage.*

**6. What did the Vikings use before any other sailors did?**
   A. wood
   B. strakes
   C. sails
   D. oars

*HINT: This question asks you to recall a detail from the passage. If you are unsure of the answer, reread the beginning of the passage.*

**7. What was the difference between early and later longboats?**
   A. Later longboats had more sails than earlier longboats.
   B. Earlier longboats were heavier and shorter than later longboats.
   C. Later longboats had higher sides than earlier longboats.
   D. Earlier longboats were handmade, and later longboats were not.

*HINT: This question asks you to think about information from the passage. If you are unsure of the answer, skim the passage looking for a comparison of the boats from earlier times to those made later.*

**8. What does the word "fierce" mean as it is used in paragraph 12?**
   A. tough
   B. sore
   C. kind
   D. honest

*HINT: This question asks you to identify the meaning of the word "fierce." Are there any clues to the word's meaning in the paragraph?*

**FOR THE OPEN-ENDED QUESTION BELOW, REMEMBER TO:**
- Pay attention to what the question is asking you.
- Be sure to answer everything the question asks you.
- Fully explain what you mean by your answer.
- Use details from the story/passage.

9. The Vikings were the first sailors in history to use a keel. They were also one of the first groups to explore a great distance away from land.
   - Explain the importance and purpose of the keel.
   - What might be one reason why the Vikings needed the keel to successfully further their explorations?

   Use information from the passage to support your response.

# CHAPTER 4

# Expanding the Text
## Predicting Meaning, Questioning, and Identifying Literary Conventions

**RL.5.6: NARRATOR OR SPEAKER'S POINT OF VIEW**
**RI.5.8: AUTHOR'S REASONS AND EVIDENCE**

Have you ever tried to guess how a story you were reading would end? Perhaps you were reading a detective story and you tried to figure out which character had committed a crime. If so, you were trying to predict the ending. To **predict** means to guess or to say what will happen in the future. When we predict, we make predictions. Often we make predictions based on known facts or past experience. In this chapter you will work on predicting.

One can predict things other than events or endings. You may be asked to **predict meaning**. Sometimes it is not clear what an author means. In fact, it may seem as if the author's words could mean more than one thing. In these situations it is up to you, the reader, to try to guess what the author is really getting at.

**Questioning** is another important comprehension skill. Asking questions about a text before, while, and after reading helps a reader check his or her understanding about what has happened so far in a story; confirm or create new predictions; and make personal connections to a text.

## YOU TRY IT

**What Would You Do?**
You see a book sitting on your neighbor's desk. The title of the book is *"The Odd World of Jimmy the Cat."* You try to predict what the book is about to decide if you want to read it or not. How do you develop your prediction?
• Do you flip through the pages and look at the illustrations?
• Do you read the title and think about what it might mean?
• Do you read the first few pages of the book?

One good way to check your understanding of a story is to stop from time-to-time to ask yourself, "Is my prediction right?" If it is not right, what is different?

## How can I predict meaning?

You can predict meaning by anticipating what the author is going to say as the story goes on.

One of the ways to do this is to relate what you are reading to your own life. You may think of an experience of your own or one that a friend had that was similar to the situation in the story.

For example, if the story is describing moving to a new town, you may remember a time when your family moved. You may relate the characters in the story to people you actually know, both the good friends you left behind and the new friends you made. As you think about your own experiences, you may come up with an idea of what will happen next in the story based on what has happened to you.

Even if you have never had the experience that the characters in the story are having, you can still think about the story and imagine what may happen.

## LET'S TRY IT TOGETHER

**DIRECTIONS**   Read the story/passage and together we will discuss the questions.

# The Package

Oscar had been waiting for this box to arrive. Its contents could mean the difference between utter failure and outstanding success. Oscar examined the contents of the package. He could not believe his luck! This was just too much to accept.   ■

## What could the author mean?

In the paragraph, the author states that the character Oscar "could not believe his luck," and that whatever was in the box was "just too much to accept." Based on this short paragraph, it seems that the author could mean two things by this. It could be that the author means that Oscar could not believe his GOOD luck. In that case it would seem that he felt the "outstanding success" was "too much to accept." In other words he was overwhelmed by this fortunate outcome.

However, the author could mean that Oscar could not believe his BAD luck. In that case it would seem that he was angered by the "utter failure" for which he felt himself destined.

## What is the goal of questioning?

You know how important it is to think about what you are reading. A good way to do this is to think of questions about the text. This is called questioning.

**Questioning** means to seek information.

The goal of any question you ask would be to learn more about the passage or the author's purpose.

Sometimes you may want to ask a question of a character in the story. At other times, you may wish to ask the author a question. Of course, you shouldn't expect the character or author to answer you. The purpose of the question is to make yourself try to think of the answer.

## How do I ask good questions?

Asking a good question is not easy. You have to carefully think before you ask a question.

**Here are tips for asking good questions:**
- Think about what you want to know.
  *Sometimes you may not be able to ask more than one question. You should choose each question carefully to make sure that you will find out what you want to know.*
- Be sure to word your question carefully.
  *If the question is unclear, you may not get the answer you're looking for.*

## Why is it important to understand what I read?

Sometimes what you read is complicated and hard to understand.

When this happens, it is probably a good idea to pause while you read parts of the story and ask yourself if you've understood what the story is saying so far. Then go on and continue reading.

Understanding what you read is important when you are trying to explain what you have read and when you are asked questions about the text.

## What questions would have to do with understanding text?

**Here are questions that you may be asked that would require you to make something more clear:**
• What is the theme or central idea of the passage?
• Is this true?
• How does the author think or feel about the topic?
• How did the writer approach the topic?
• Who do you think is the audience the author was trying to reach?
• Compare and contrast by telling what is the same and what is different in the text.

## How can I predict what will happen?

**Predicting** means expecting something to happen, telling what is going to happen, and being prepared for the outcome.

Here, too, your personal experience will help you. If you have been in a similar situation yourself, you may be able to guess what will happen next in a story.

You can also use context clues to make predictions about the story. This skill is almost always used in open-ended questions.

## How can I predict the outcome?

Another thing to do when you read is to predict the outcome. Here, too, you may be able to draw on your own experience to help you. If that's not possible, you may be able to imagine what you would have done in the situation.

Sometimes you will be reading only part of a story and you will have to answer a question about what will happen next. You will be asked to predict the outcome.

## LET'S TRY IT TOGETHER

**DIRECTIONS**   Read the story/passage and together we will discuss the questions.

# Walking to School

Walking a little more than a mile to school each day took our group past several blocks of neighborhood houses. Then we took a path through a wooded area. Emerging from the woods, we found ourselves at the very edge of the school playground. Then we all dispersed to our different classrooms. The year that my little brother started school, I was in the fifth grade.

I really didn't want to walk him with us older kids. But one morning, while I was talking excitedly about a famous visitor to our school with one of my classmates, I lost sight of my little brother. When I turned to look, I could see him far off in the distance. His little legs were going as fast as they could IN THE OTHER DIRECTION! ▪

## What will happen next in the story?

**Here are some questions you may ask in order to predict the outcome of the story:**
- Will the author risk being late for school by leaving her friends and the other neighborhood children and chasing after her brother?
- If she doesn't, what will she do instead?
- How would you write the next part of this story?

You might guess that a responsible older sister would chase after her little brother and bring him back. If she had thought about it soon enough, she might have asked her friends to notify both teachers about the situation when they got to school.

## LET'S TRY IT TOGETHER

**DIRECTIONS** Read the story/passage and together we will discuss the questions.

# Going to the Fair

Joy had learned how to bake from her mother. Her father preferred pies to cakes, so Joy had had a lot of practice baking pies—apple, peach, banana cream, lemon meringue, and other kinds. Even though she was eleven years old, Joy really had become an expert baker.

After Joy's apple pie was served at a family gathering, her Aunt Terry said that the pie was so delicious that it should be entered in the baking competition at the county fair. Joy was a little shy about doing this, but all her relatives were encouraging her. The deadline to register was the following week, and Joy just wasn't sure what to do. ∎

1. **What do you think Joy will do? If she does decide to take her pie to the fair, how will she do in the competition?**

**How do I guess what is going to happen?**

It's fun to take the story in your own direction. However, you should map out what you are going to say before you write it.

**Here are questions to ask yourself before writing:**
- What do I know about the characters?
- Where did the passage leave off?
- Have I ever had a similar experience?
- Are there hints in the story about what will happen next?
- How do I want my story to progress?
- What will happen first?
- What will happen next and last?

## What are figures of speech?

One of the many ways writers improve their work is by using **figures of speech**. One type of figure of speech that writers include is imagery. **Imagery** is the use of figurative language to represent ideas, objects, or actions.

**Example:**
Her smile was so beautiful, it sparkled like diamonds.

In this sentence the author is using imagery to help the reader imagine how beautiful the girl's smile looked.

Two common types of imagery that you may have already learned about are **similes** and **metaphors**. Both smiles and metaphors compare two different things in a creative and imaginative way. In this chapter, you will learn about three more kinds of figures of speech: **hyperbole**, **onomatopoeia**, and **idioms**. First, we will review similes and metaphors.

## What is a simile?

A **simile** is a figure of speech where something is compared to something else, using the words *as* or *like*. In a simile, two unlike things are explicitly compared.

**Read these examples of similes.**
- The sidewalk is as slippery as greased glass.
- The snow was as thick as a blanket.
- Melanie is as good as gold.
- My mother's heart is as soft as a feather pillow.
- The tiny little girl is as delicate as a flower.
- The ground this summer is as dry as a bone.

## Now it's your turn!

Try to write some similes yourself. Remember that similes have to compare two things. You also have to use either the word *as* or the word *like* in each one.

_____

_____

_____

_____

_____

## What is a metaphor?

A **metaphor** is also a comparison. However, it does not use the words *as* or *like* in the same way a simile does.

A metaphor uses an expression or a word to refer to something it does not literally mean in order to suggest a similarity.

Here is a metaphor from the great playwright William Shakespeare's "Romeo and Juliet":

"But, soft! what light… and Juliet is the sun!"

## What would be an example?

**Read these other examples of metaphors.**

• My uncle is a tiger when he's angry.
• The rat didn't have a chance; our cat, a bolt of lightning, caught him.
• The chef's dish was exploding with flavor. (verb metaphor)
• Her smile was a ray of sunlight.

## Now it's your turn!

Try to write some metaphors yourself. Keep in mind that sometimes a very complicated thing is compared to a simpler thing in order to make the more complicated thing easier to understand.

_____

_____

_____

_____

_____

# What is hyperbole?

Has anyone ever said to you, "I have told you a million times… "? Have you ever said, "I could sleep for a year"? These are both examples of hyperbole, the use of exaggeration to emphasize a feeling, an effort, or a reaction.

**Hyperbole** is the figure of speech where deliberate exaggeration is used for effect.

**Here are some examples of hyperbole.**
- His feet were as big as a boat.
- I nearly died laughing.
- This is like waiting an eternity.
- I'm so hungry I could eat a horse.

# Now it's your turn!

Try to write some of your own examples of hyperbole. Remember that you are deliberately exaggerating something to emphasize a feeling, an effort, or a reaction.

_____

_____

_____

_____

_____

## What is onomatopoeia?

**Meow! Woof! Bang! Thud! Crash! Zip!**

When you see these words, do you know right away what they mean? These are sound-effect words or noise words.

The figure of speech called **onomatopoeia** is the use of words that imitate the sound of the objects they name.

In onomatopoeia, the sounds literally make the meaning. The word is the Greek word for "name making."

**Here are some other examples of onomatopoeia:**
- The fly buzzed past.
- The owl hooted.
- Jerry clattered and clanged as he washed the dishes.
- The burgers sizzled on the grill.

**Here is a poem using onomatopoeia by Eve Merriam:**

The rusty spigot
sputters,
utters
a splutter,
spatters a smattering of drops,
gashes wider;
slash,
splatters,
scatters,
spurts,
finally stops sputtering
and plash!
gushes rushes splashes
clear water dashes.

## Now it's your turn!

Try to write some of your own examples of onomatopoeia. Remember, for each one, to use a word that imitates a noise or an action. Try to "hear" in your mind the sound of each example as you write.

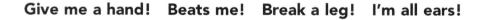

## What is an idiom?

**Give me a hand!   Beats me!   Break a leg!   I'm all ears!**

An **idiom** is a way of speaking that is natural to native speakers of a certain language. It is a form of expression peculiar to one language.

In English, we have many, many idioms. This is one of the reasons why it is so difficult for someone from another country to learn English.

Idioms are made up of ordinary words, but the meanings are very different from the usual meanings.  Surely you hear some idioms every day, and probably you use them, too.

While you may already know what the idioms above mean, here they are along with some others:

| IDIOM | MEANING |
|---|---|
| give someone a hand | help someone |
| Beats me. | I have no idea. |
| Break a leg! | Good luck! |
| antsy | restless, impatient, tired of waiting |
| be all ears | eager to hear what someone has to say |
| call it a day | stop work for the day |
| down in the dumps | unhappy, feeling "blue" |

## Now it's your turn!

Try to write some of your own examples of idioms. Write a sentence for each one. Remember that an idiom uses ordinary words and gives them different meanings.

_____

_____

_____

_____

_____

_____

Why do I see *italics*, CAPITALS and **bold** lettering when I read?

You already know that sometimes authors use special kinds of type in their writing. They do this for different reasons. Examples of special type are *italics*, all CAPITAL letters, and **bold** lettering.

One of the reasons authors use special type is **emphasis**. The author wants the reader to pay special attention to a word in special type and to be able to understand why this word is important and why the author is emphasizing it in this part of the story.

Another reason is to make the writing clearer and more precise. **Read these three examples.**

**1** Janice and her friend Sue were pretending to be grown up. It was summer and they were playing in the attic. In an old wardrobe, they found dresses, hats, and shoes in styles they had never seen before.

The girls started trying things on. Soon they were giggling at each other. Sue, wearing a long blue velvet dress and a wide, flowery hat, was acting as if she were royalty. Janice laughed and pointed at her, "Look at *you*!"

**2** Michael left the dentist's office and went to his car. He started the motor and eased into traffic. Immediately, he heard a loud rumbling noise, so he pulled over.

He got out of the car and walked around it. He was late for a meeting, and didn't want any thing to delay him. Then          Michael saw it. There was the problem—a FLAT tire!

**3** **How to Prune a Rose Bush**
1. Use clean, sharp tools.
2. Look at the overall plant, but begin pruning from the base of the plant.
3. Prune to open the center of the plant to light and air circulation.
4. Make your cuts at a 45-degree angle, about 1/4-inch above a bud that is facing toward the outside of the plant.
5. Make sure it is a clean cut (not ragged).
6. Remove all broken, dead, dying or diseased wood. (Any branches that look dry, shriveled or black.)

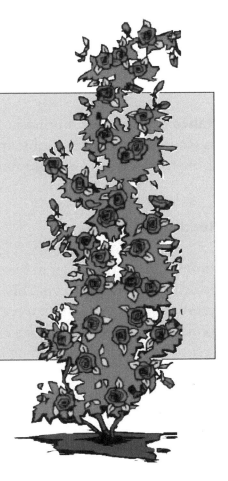

## Now it's your turn!

Write one of your own sentences for each kind of emphasis: *italics*, all CAPITAL letters, and **bold** lettering.

_____

_____

_____

_____

## How can I use italics?

**Italics** are used for emphasis, but have other uses as well. A person's thoughts may be in italics, while spoken words will be in quotation marks.

**Read this example:**

Johnny slid as far down in his seat as he could. The principal had come to visit his class, and was asking questions. Some students were eager to answer. All Johnny could think was, *I hope that she doesn't call on me. I get so nervous when something like this happens.*

The principal asked, "What are some good things that happened for you during this school year?" His friend Sam—who didn't have Johnny's problem—stood up and said, "Thank you for letting us go to the zoo last month. I saw some animals there that I had never seen before."

## How else can I use italics?

**Italics are used for the titles of books, magazines, newspapers, etc. Here are some examples:**

**Books**
*Oh, the Places You'll Go!* by Dr. Seuss
*The Wonderful Wizard of Oz* by L. Frank Baum

**Magazines**
*U.S. News and World Report*
*Time*
*Sports Illustrated*

**Newspapers**
*Chicago Tribune*
*Atlanta Journal-Constitution*
*New York Times*

**Italics are used for the names of vehicles, e.g., ships, spacecraft.**

**Ships**
*USS Constitution*
*Titanic*
*RMS Queen Elizabeth 2*

**Spacecraft**
*Mariner 2*
*Challenger*
*Apollo*

**Another use of italics is for words as reproduced sounds (onomatopoeia). Here are some examples using italics:**

"*Woof! Woof!*" The large dog greeted the little boy.

When bees buzz they make a sound like *bzzzzzzzzz.*

*Clunk! Crash!* The ball first hit the side of the house and then it broke the window and fell to the living room floor.

## YOU TRY IT

| DIRECTIONS INTRODUCTION | Read this story/passage and answer the questions that follow. This story describes how experiences during a family vacation help two brothers understand and appreciate many different things worth remembering, preserving, and protecting. |
| --- | --- |

# So Many Things Worth Keeping

Miguel and Carlos Garcia scurried around, both carrying various items of clothing. They heaped them onto their beds. Their once neatly organized to-do lists had many cross-outs and hastily scribbled changes. They were running out of time. They had to be all packed tonight because their flight was going to leave at 7:00 a.m. the following day.

"Mom," Carlos pleaded, "have you seen my green sweatshirt? I've looked everywhere and I can't find it!"

"Bottom left-hand drawer in your dresser. I put it there yesterday," she replied, sighing. "I'll be right there to help you. I want to be sure you have enough of the essentials packed." For Juanita Garcia, the boys' mother, essentials were things like socks, underwear, and sweaters. She certainly didn't count electronic games and CDs.

Each of the brothers had his own suitcase with wheels, just the right size to maneuver through airports. Packing for a three-week trip wasn't easy. However, their mother had found some airtight packing bags, which the boys could stuff and zip their clothes into. As they rolled each bag—swoosh!—the air went out through a valve like air escaping from a tire. Their clothes wouldn't be squashed then and would take up less than half of their original space.

When Pedro Garcia arrived home, the major packing had been completed. However, the boys' father had brought several unusual objects with him. They were round tubes several feet long. What in the world could he have? His wife had a funny smile on her face. The boys recognized that look. Obviously, what was in the packages was no surprise to her.

"Here's one for you, Carlos, and one for you, Miguel. Open them. I'm sure they'll come in handy on our trip," Mr. Garcia said.

The boys ripped off the wrapping paper and pried open the round caps at one end of the metal tubes. Out slipped beautiful two-piece fishing rods. In another smaller package, they each found spinning reels and monofilament fishing line. The boys were beaming with excitement. It seemed that everyone was talking, smiling, and laughing at once.

"What about you and Mom? What are you going to use?" Miguel inquired.

Their dad chuckled. "You don't think I'd let you two have all the fun. I've got equipment for us, too. I just left it out in the hall. I bought special carrying bags for the tubes, so we ought to be able to take them on board the plane. If not, I'm sure the airline has ways we can ship them safely."

Even though they had to be up early, no one really needed the alarm clock to wake up. Showers, dressing, and breakfast were over in no time. Last-minute toiletry articles were packed. Suitcases were zipped up and locked. For the umpteenth time, their dad checked the tickets and travel documents.

Their mom made sure that all windows were locked, most appliances unplugged, and the faucets firmly turned off. The airport limousine arrived right on time for the half-hour ride to the airport. Their vacation was about to begin.

In order to have more time to see the wonders of Colorado, Mr. and Mrs. Garcia decided to fly to Denver and rent a camper. Each family member had listed so many places he or she wanted to visit that even three weeks wouldn't be enough time to see everything.

When the plane landed at Denver International Airport, the Garcias claimed their baggage and went to retrieve their rented vehicle. They stowed their luggage in the camper and headed for a nearby campground. The family noticed right away that it was a bit hard to breathe. The Garcias planned to stay in Denver for a few days to get used to the altitude.

**✔ CHECK FOR UNDERSTANDING**

Based on the gift the boys received from their parents, what kind of trip do you think the family is about to go on?

The first place they visited was the U.S. Mint. Miguel and Carlos loved learning about the process of making money. They learned that two million coins are made each hour. Next, they went to the State Capitol where they discovered how Denver got its nickname, "The Mile High City." The fifteenth step on the west entrance is exactly one mile above sea level. At the Museum of Nature and Science, they watched scientists work in the fossil lab. Later, they viewed sharks as they walked through a tube at the aquarium. Finally, they left for Rocky Mountain National Park.

"These Rockies are the Great Divide," Mr. Garcia told his sons as they drove toward the park.

"What does that mean, Dad?" Carlos asked.

"Well, it marks where our rivers flow either east or west," he said. "On the western side, the slopes are gentle and the rain that falls there creates lush meadows and lots of streams and lakes."

Miguel inquired, "Is the eastern side like that, too?"

"No, Miguel," he replied. "On that side, the mountains are steep with rocky gorges 2,000 and 3,000 feet deep. You'll see some of this as we travel through Rocky Mountain National Park. There are 78 peaks reaching 12,000 feet or higher in the park and there are even some glaciers there in the high mountain canyons."

"Imagine having a snowball fight in July!" Miguel exclaimed.

Suddenly, Mrs. Garcia turned to her husband. "Pedro, pull off the road. I just saw some Rocky Mountain sheep on that hillside."

They all got out to look at the sheep with their big curled horns. It was easy to see how they got the nickname "bighorn sheep." Mrs. Garcia told the boys, "This park is a wildlife sanctuary where animals are protected."

"What kinds of animals are here, besides the bighorn sheep?" Carlos asked.

Mr. Garcia told them, "If we keep our eyes open, we may see elk, deer, coyotes, and black bears. There are bobcats, mountain lions, and other animals, too, but we aren't likely to see them."

As they drove through the park, they talked about the parks and forests set aside to protect plants and animals. "It's important to our ecology to have these lands protected, too," Mrs. Garcia explained.

"It certainly is," Miguel agreed, nodding. "Protected lands help keep chemicals and pollutants out of our water system. Clean water is important for us, for plants, and for animals to be healthy. It wouldn't do us any good to catch fish if they were sick from polluted water. We wouldn't be able to eat them."

"That would be terrible," Carlos exclaimed. "It's not so much that I want to eat them, but we wouldn't get to use our new fishing gear!"

His parents laughed. "You have nothing to worry about. When we get our licenses, we'll ask about a good fishing lake. Then, we'll buy lures and maybe some live bait."

The family enjoyed three days of camping at Lake Granby. Fishing went slowly until another fisherman shared his secret bait with them. Then, they caught enough fish for supper each night; they released the rest. Mr. Garcia fried the fish they kept over a small campfire. They all agreed that these were the best fish they had ever eaten.

The rest of the vacation flew by. They visited an abandoned gold mine and a ghost town. Then, they enjoyed a chuck wagon dinner at a cattle ranch. Other highlights were a trip on the cog railroad to the top of Pike's Peak, a stop at the Buffalo Bill Museum, and a tour of the Air Force Academy. Too soon, it was time to leave Colorado.

On the flight home, the family talked about what they had experienced. Carlos summed up their feelings when he announced, "Now I understand why it's so important to protect our environment. I never knew just how beautiful our country is. It would be a shame if it weren't around for others to see." ■

**1. What made packing for the trip difficult for Miguel and Carlos?**

  A.  They couldn't decide which CDs to take.

  B.  They were running out of time to pack.

  C.  Their mother didn't think they needed help.

  D.  They had to share one suitcase together.

*HINT: This question asks you to recall a detail from the passage. If you are unsure of the answer, reread the beginning of the passage.*

**2. What is Denver's nickname?**

  A.  The Great Divide

  B.  Bighorn Sheep

  C.  The Mile High City

  D.  Pike's Peak

*HINT: This question asks you to recall a detail from the passage. If you are unsure of the answer, skim the passage looking for a mention of Denver.*

**3. What helped the Garcias to catch fish?**

  A.  a fisherman's special bait

  B.  an extra set of fishing poles

  C.  a new fishing license

  D.  a herd of bighorn sheep

*HINT: This question asks you to recall a detail from the passage. If you are unsure of the answer, reread the end of the passage.*

**4. What is this passage mostly about?**

  A.  the best place to go fishing

  B.  things to do while in Denver

  C.  a family vacation to Colorado

  D.  how to pack for a three-week trip

*HINT: This question asks you to identify the central idea of the passage. Think about what you have read. What do you think the author was trying to tell you about?*

**5. Read the following sentence from the passage.**

" 'I want to be sure you have enough of the *essentials* packed.' "

**What does the word "essentials" mean in this sentence?**

A. suitcases

B. fun toys

C. needed items

D. food and drink

HINT: *This question asks you to identify the meaning of the word "essentials." Are there any clues to the word's meaning in the sentence?*

**6. How do the boys react when they open the fishing poles?**

A. confused

B. eager

C. bored

D. afraid

HINT: *This question asks you to draw a conclusion based on the passage. Can you remember what the boys said or did when they got the fishing poles? If you are unsure of the answer, reread the beginning of the passage.*

**7. What important lesson did Carlos and Miguel learn while on vacation?**

A. They should visit Colorado more often.

B. They should learn from a fisherman how to fish.

C. They should pack extra sweaters for trips.

D. They should try to appreciate nature.

HINT: *This question asks you to think about information from the passage. If you are unsure of the answer, skim the passage and think about a lesson the boys might have learned.*

**8. How is the eastern side of the Rocky Mountains different from the western side?**

A. There are steep, rocky gorges on the eastern side.

B. There are lush meadows on the eastern side.

C. There is a lot of rainfall on the eastern side.

D. There are many lakes and streams on the eastern side.

HINT: *This question asks you to recall a detail from the passage. If you are unsure of the answer, look over the passage. You should be looking for a mention of the Rocky Mountains.*

**9. How is this passage organized?**
   A. by describing how the Garcias looked at a set of pictures
   B. by describing what the Garcias did as their trip happened
   C. by describing each member of the family's memories
   D. by describing what each person of the family wants to do

*HINT: This question asks you to think about the text. Why do you think the author wrote this passage the way he did?*

**10. How would the Garcias most likely feel if wildlife protections were eliminated?**
   A. They wouldn't be too concerned about the fish.
   B. They would be concerned about the fish's safety.
   C. They wouldn't know of any problems for the fish.
   D. They would tell people not to worry about the fish.

*HINT: This question asks you to draw a conclusion based on the passage. Based on what you have read, how do you think the Garcias feel about wildlife protection?*

**FOR THE OPEN-ENDED QUESTION BELOW, REMEMBER TO:**
• Pay attention to what the question is asking you.
• Be sure to answer everything the question asks you.
• Fully explain what you mean by your answer.
• Use details from the story/passage.

11. In the story, the family enjoyed some activities related to nature and some related to civilization.
    • List and describe four activities they enjoyed that were related to nature.
    • List and describe four activities they enjoyed that were related to civilization.
    Use information from the story to support your response.

**FOR THE OPEN-ENDED QUESTION BELOW, REMEMBER TO:**
- Pay attention to what the question is asking you.
- Be sure to answer everything the question asks you.
- Fully explain what you mean by your answer.
- Use details from the story/passage.

12. The author used fishing in a few important ways to tell this story.
    - **Explain the importance of fishing to the story and to the boys themselves.**

    **Use information from the story to support your response.**

## YOU TRY IT

| | |
|---|---|
| **DIRECTIONS**<br>**INTRODUCTION** | Read this story/passage and answer the questions that follow. This passage discusses a famous archeologist and the fascinating work he and others do to discover information about the past. |

# Under the Desert Sands

*A cloud of dusty desert sand drifts upward through the shaft that leads down to a recently excavated tomb. Below, Egypt's leading archeologist, Dr. Zahi Hawass, moves a loose large jagged rock. It's blocking the entrance to another, unexplored section of this ancient tomb. The rock comes out, leaving a small opening. Hawass struggles to crawl through a space barely large enough for his body, much less the TV camera he takes with him. He wants us to be the first to see what he uncovers. "You never know what the sands of the desert will reveal," Dr. Hawass says with a smile.*

We're in the Valley of the Golden Mummies, where over two hundred bodies covered with gold have already been unearthed. That's the largest number of mummies ever discovered at a single site. Dr. Zahi, as the famous scientist is known in Egypt, leads us through a series of chambers cut into the rock. Everywhere we look, there are mummies and artifacts. They tell a story about ancient Egypt and the people who lived…and died…here.

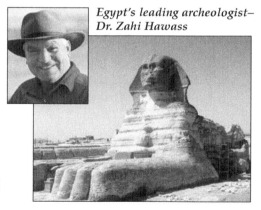

*Egypt's leading archeologist–*
*Dr. Zahi Hawass*

Dr. Zahi's crew strains to move the lid of a 70-ton sarcophagus so we can get a peek at the mummy inside—someone who walked on the hot desert sand above us thousands of years ago.

### The Rich and the Poor

Archaeologists like Dr. Zahi literally touch history. They sift through sites and dig through dunes to learn more about people of the past. They may be the first to touch the face of a golden mummy buried in a desert tomb for thousands of years or the first to hold a golden coin that fell to the ground 2,000 years ago.

So far, Dr. Zahi's team has unearthed more than 250 gilded mummies. He believes they could eventually find up to 10,000!

These mummies, Dr. Zahi believes, had been rich or middle class people. He's also working on a project with mummies of working class people—those who built the pyramids in which Egypt's ancient rulers, or pharaohs, were buried.

**CHECK FOR UNDERSTANDING**

What else do you think archaeologists might be able to learn about ancient people from studying artifacts found in the ground?

These were found in 1990, when an American tourist's horse tripped over part of a wall near the Sphinx at Giza. Dr. Zahi's team was called and they discovered the tombs of the pyramid builders.

Among their findings were construction workers whose bones showed stress from years of heavy lifting. They also found skilled craftsmen in tombs filled with drawings and hieroglyphs. The cemetery of the pyramid builders is filled with different-shaped tombs erected between 2551–2323 B.C.

Another amazing find, although not a tomb, was the world's oldest bakery. Well, I guess you could say it was a tomb for old crumbs because it was still stocked with cooking tools and dough-making equipment! Dr. Zahi believes the bakery made bread for the more than 20,000 hungry pyramid builders. And it's possible that the bread was responsible for the bad teeth and gums of some ancient Egyptians. Rocks used to grind the grain left behind bits of sand and stone. So the bread was good… but gritty! Over time, it could wear down the teeth and hurt the gums.

Who knows what Dr. Zahi and his team will find next at Giza or in the Valley of the Golden Mummies. As we speak, they're at work searching for tombs… and more. ∎

**1. In the second paragraph which two words are used as synonyms?**

   A. largest and single

   B. unearthed and discovered

   C. chambers and artifacts

   D. famous and scientist

*HINT: This question asks you which two words are synonyms. Remember, synonyms mean two words that mean the same thing. Which two words in this paragraph mean the same thing?*

**2. What is the author's purpose in writing this passage?**

   A. to persuade the reader

   B. to entertain the reader

   C. to inform the reader

   D. to convince the reader

*HINT: This question is about author's purpose. Why do you think the author decided to write this passage?*

**3. What is a "pharaoh"?**

   A. a gold-covered mummy

   B. a person who made pyramids

   C. a type of drawing on a tomb

   D. a ruler from ancient Egypt

*HINT: This question asks you to figure out the meaning of a vocabulary word. Look back at the word in the passage. Does the context around the word help you figure out its meaning?*

**4. Why is Dr. Hawass famous in Egypt?**

   A. He was the one who found a wall near the Sphinx

   B. He discovered that bread in Egypt is very gritty.

   C. He has helped Egyptians learn about their past.

   D. He crawled through caves with a TV camera.

*HINT: This question asks about a main idea of this passage. After reading this entire passage think about what Dr. Hawass does that makes him famous in Egypt.*

**5. What is Dr. Hawass' goal when he and his team go on their digs?**

   A. to find out what the pyramids were made out of

   B. to uncover and take as much gold as they can get

   C. to learn what life was like thousands of years ago

   D. to document their discovery on TV for people to see

*HINT: This question asks about a character's motivation in this selection. What words does the author use to explain why Dr. Hawass goes on his different digs?*

**6. What unexpected thing does Dr. Hawass discover?**

   A. many gold pieces

   B. an ancient bakery

   C. a wall near the Sphinx

   D. two large sand dunes

*HINT: This question asks you to evaluate information from the passage. Which discovery does Dr. Hawass make that he was not originally trying to discover?*

**7. Which from the passage supports the idea that Dr. Zahi Hawass is success at his job?**

   A. These mummies, Dr. Zahi believes, had been rich or middle class people.

   B. So far, Dr. Zahi's team has unearthed more than 250 gilded mummies.

   C. Dr. Zahi believes the bakery made bread for the more than 20,000 hungry pyramid builders.

   D. Who know what Dr. Zahi and his team will find next at Giza or in the Valley of the Golden Mummies.

*HINT: This question is asking you to find a supporting detail. His job is discovering mummies and tombs. Which details supports the idea that Dr. Hawass has discovered a lot of mummies?*

**8. Why does the author include and italicize the first paragraph?**

   A. to list the vocabulary words for the reader

   B. to give the reader details about the author

   C. to tell the reader where they can find Egypt

   D. to help paint a picture in the reader's mind

*HINT: This question asks about the author's purpose for include a particular paragraph. Reread the first paragraph. What is the author doing for the reader in this paragraph?*

**9. Where might you find this selection?**
   A. a magazine about famous discoverers
   B. a book about how the sphinx was built
   C. a fictional chapter book about mummies
   D. an encyclopedia article about golden tombs

*HINT: This question asks where you might find this passage. Why might someone read this passage? What is the passage mainly about?*

**10. What does Dr. Hawass mean when he says, "You never know what the sands of the desert will reveal?"**
   A. if he look hard he can see pictures in the sand
   B. he gets scared every time he goes on a new dig
   C. every dig he goes on is a new adventure for him
   D. he must know what he is looking for on each dig

*HINT: This question asks you to interpret implicit meaning. Remember implicit meaning is a meaning that is not written out in words. What do you think Dr. Hawass means when he says this?*

**FOR THE OPEN-ENDED QUESTION BELOW, REMEMBER TO:**
- Pay attention to what the question is asking you.
- Be sure to answer everything the question asks you.
- Fully explain what you mean by your answer.
- Use details from the story/passage.

11. This passage describes many things Dr. Hawass discovers.

- **Identify two things that Dr. Hawass discovers in this passage.**

- **Explain why each discovery was very important.**

**Use information from the story to support your response.**

**FOR THE OPEN-ENDED QUESTION BELOW, REMEMBER TO:**
• Pay attention to what the question is asking you.
• Be sure to answer everything the question asks you.
• Fully explain what you mean by your answer.
• Use details from the story/passage.

12. **This passage introduces the reader to an interesting scientist.**

   • **Explain two character traits that describe Dr. Zahi Hawass.**

   • **Use details, or examples, from the selection that support each character trait.**

   **Use information from the story to support your response.**

## YOU TRY IT

| **DIRECTIONS** **INTRODUCTION** | Read this passage and answer the questions that follow. In the beginning of World War II, the American government moved all Japanese Americans to special camps. They were kept there under guard for four years. Today, this action is remembered as the "Time of Shame" in our history. |
|---|---|

# The Relocation of Japanese Americans

In 1941, when Japan bombed the coast of Hawaii at Pearl Harbor, the lives of Japanese Americans quickly changed. The U.S. government forced them to leave their homes. They were sent to internment camps.[1] These were far from the Pacific Ocean. The camps were intended to prevent Japanese Americans from helping the country that had suddenly become our enemy: Japan.

During the 1920s and 1930s, many Japanese families came to the United States. They settled on the west coast in the states of California, Oregon, and Washington.

Like the thousands of immigrants before them, the Japanese established themselves in society. They bought homes, started businesses, and raised families.

After the bombing at Pearl Harbor, many newspapers forgot about fairness. Headlines said that people of Japanese descent had to leave. Articles written at the time stated that if the Japanese Americans were not moved, they would help the enemy. Although

[1]**internment camp** *a large detention center created for political opponents, enemy aliens, specific ethnic or religious groups, civilians of a critical war-zone, or other groups of people, usually during a war*

these words were untrue, people were scared. Many Americans agreed that the Japanese Americans should be sent to the internment camps.

This action by our government stunned many people. The Japanese people had lived in our country for years. Many were United States citizens. The Bill of Rights said that what had been done to them as a result of Pearl Harbor was wrong. Most people felt that the camps were unfair. Yet, the Japanese Americans were kept there. In fact, even though the U.S. was at war with both Germany and Japan, only the Japanese Americans were treated this way.

## CHECK FOR UNDERSTANDING

Why do you think some people were feeling so angry toward Japanese Americans?

President Roosevelt agreed with those Americans who feared the threat that the Japanese Americans might have posed to our country. He signed Executive Order 9066, which allowed the government to move them into camps. The military acted quickly. Often, the Japanese-American people had only three days' warning before they were moved. Many were forced to sell their homes and businesses, suffering huge financial losses. Others stored their belongings. Each person was allowed to take only one suitcase to the camps.

After spending a few weeks in control centers, the Japanese Americans were put on trains and not told where they were going.

There were ten internment camps in remote parts of the U.S. Over 120,000 *Nikkei*—Americans of Japanese descent and immigrants who had come to the United States from Japan—were moved to these camps. The

camps were very restrictive; with drastic measures to prevent escape. Barbed-wire fences surrounded each camp. Guard towers lined the sides. Soldiers patrolled the grounds. People were not allowed close to the fences. It was very much like prison.

Life in the camps was boring and unenjoyable. Food was served in large buildings. There was no place for a person to be alone. Despite the hardship, they soon brought order to their lives. Schools were started, gardens were grown, and clubs were organized. They tried to make life as normal as possible.

*Figure 1*

*Figure 1* shows what a typical camp room looked like. Each family was given one small room. In this room they had a stove, army cots, blankets, and one electric light. Later, the people were allowed to build furniture.

By 1943, things had begun to change and, in some ways, improve. Farms near the camps needed workers to help them save their crops. Many men and women were overseas helping or fighting in the war, and many women at home were working factory jobs or helping in other ways toward the war effort. Some of the Japanese people living in the camps were then given the opportunity to take these farm jobs. The wages were very low, but it gave them a way to escape from the camps for a short time.

Soon the people living in the camps started to enjoy more freedoms. Some Japanese-American students began to attend college. The army asked the young Japanese-Americans to enlist; some volunteered and served bravely. However, most did not because they felt that the military had treated them unfairly. In spite of the freedoms, internment camps still remained. Anyone who wanted to leave them had to first get permission.

In 1944, things changed again. Some people were allowed to leave the camps. They were ordered to settle in midwestern or eastern states. In January 1945, the U.S. government closed the camps, stating that the Japanese were no longer a threat to the country. The 80,000 people still held there at that time were told that they could return home.

Unfortunately, returning home was not such a simple thing. The Japanese Americans had lost almost everything they had left behind. Most families had to start all over again. Sadly, the government offered little aid for them except that they were given transportation back home.

In 1988, President Ronald Reagan signed the Redress Bill. It was an apology to the Japanese for what the United States had done. It had taken over 40 years for this bill to become law. Later, each family affected by the internment camp ordeal received $20,000. The money was meant to repay them for what they lost during their relocation. They received an apology letter for the internment, which said that the rights of all people would be upheld in the future. ■

1. **What is this passage mostly about?**
   A. the treatment of Japanese Americans after the bombing of Pearl Harbor
   B. planning an attack after Pearl Harbor was bombed in 1941
   C. living conditions for most Americans during World War II
   D. the best way to set up clubs and organizations in a camp

   HINT: *This question asks you to identify the central idea of the passage. Think about what you have read. What do you think the author was trying to tell you about?*

2. **"The Relocation of Japanese Americans" would be useful background reading for an oral report on**
   A. people moving to the United States.
   B. how World War II was fought in Europe with the Japanese.
   C. how the U.S. government has mistreated citizens.
   D. the beginning of the civil rights movement.

   HINT: *This question asks you to think about the passage. What is the explicit meaning of the text? If you are unsure of the answer, skim the passage.*

3. **How did people react to newspaper articles about Japanese Americans?**
   A. They were confused.
   B. They felt scared.
   C. They were unconcerned.
   D. They felt sorry.

   HINT: *This question asks you to recall a detail from the passage. If you are unsure of the answer, skim the passage, looking for how people reacted to newspaper articles about the Japanese Americans.*

4. **Where did the Japanese Americans go after being forced from their homes?**
   A. the military
   B. back to Japan
   C. coastal California
   D. control centers

   HINT: *This question asks you to recall a detail from the passage. If you are unsure of the answer, reread the middle of the passage.*

**5. Why did the Japanese Americans grow gardens and start clubs in the camps?**

   A. to make the camps seem more like home

   B. to practice farming so they could work

   C. to avoid talking with the camps' guards

   D. to avoid starving while in the camp

HINT: *This question asks you to draw a conclusion based on the passage. What reason would the Japanese Americans have to want gardens and clubs?*

**6. What did *most* Japanese Americans do after returning home?**

   A. returned to work at their old jobs

   B. started their lives all over again

   C. enlisted in the military to fight the war

   D. traveled to visit family in Japan

HINT: *This question asks you to draw a conclusion based on the passage. If you are unsure of the answer, reread the end of the passage.*

**7. When did situations finally begin to improve in the camps?**

   A. 1939

   B. 1941

   C. 1943

   D. 1988

HINT: *This question asks you to recall a detail from the passage. If you are unsure of the answer, skim the passage, looking for a date when the camps improved.*

**8. What was the importance of the Redress Bill?**

   A. It showed that Japanese Americans were treated well in the camps.

   B. It admitted that the relocation of the Japanese Americans was wrong.

   C. It attempted to stop the fighting of World War II.

   D. It ordered all citizens to report to camps immediately.

HINT: *This question asks you to draw a conclusion based on the passage. If you are unsure of the answer, reread the final paragraph of the passage.*

**9. Read the following sentence from the passage.**

"There were ten camps in *remote* parts of the U.S."

**What does the word "remote" mean in this sentence?**

A. unhappy

B. well-hidden

C. empty

D. faraway

*HINT: This question asks you to identify the meaning of the word "remote." Are there any clues to the word's meaning in the sentence?*

**10. Why did most Japanese American not fight as soldiers in World War II?**

A. They thought the military had treated them unfairly.

B. They wanted to return to the islands of Japan.

C. They were too busy working on the nearby farms.

D. They were not allowed to join the U.S. Army.

*HINT: This question asks you to recall a detail from the passage. If you are unsure of the answer, reread the end of the passage.*

**FOR THE OPEN-ENDED QUESTION BELOW, REMEMBER TO:**
• Pay attention to what the question is asking you.
• Be sure to answer everything the question asks you.
• Fully explain what you mean by your answer.
• Use details from the story/passage.

11. Some Americans supported the idea of moving the Japanese Americans to the internment camps following the bombing of Pearl Harbor.
   • **Explain why people in the United States would have stood behind the U.S. government when they made the decision to intern the Japanese Americans.**
   • **Give at least four reasons to support your explanation.**
   **Use information from the article to support your response.**

**FOR THE OPEN-ENDED QUESTION BELOW, REMEMBER TO:**
• Pay attention to what the question is asking you.
• Be sure to answer everything the question asks you.
• Fully explain what you mean by your answer.
• Use details from the story/passage.

12. Life within the internment camps is explained in this article.
   • Describe what it was like for a Japanese-American person living in an internment camp when he or she was first relocated there.
   • Include at least four examples or ideas to support your description.
   Use information from the article to support your response.

## YOU TRY IT

| DIRECTIONS INTRODUCTION | Read this passage and answer the questions that follow. Jon's family just returned from Costa Rica and decided to make a scrapbook of their trip. This passage includes excerpts from a book on how to make a photo scrapbook. |
| --- | --- |

# Making a Scrapbook

**CHECK FOR UNDERSTANDING**

Why is treasuring times spent with friends and family so important in life?

Making a photo scrapbook of a trip is a lot of fun. Scrapbooking reminds you of all the things you did on the trip. It also helps build a feeling of closeness in your family. People enjoy seeing pictures of trips and, as they look at the pictures, talking about the fun they had.

Making scrapbooks is also entertaining. You will see photos of funny things done by members of your family, and you may even discover new things you didn't know had happened on the trip. Putting a photo scrapbook together is a great family activity and often gets you talking about your next trip.

Making a scrapbook is not hard. It is made one page at a time, and as you finish each page, you put it into a binder. When you finish the last page, the scrapbook is done.

**You need the following supplies:**
• a scrapbook binder
• acid-free, lignin-free paper
• acid-free glue stick
• acid-free pen

**5** You will also need assorted colored sheets of paper. The color you use depends on the background you want for your pictures. Many people use various colors in their scrapbook. Paper for scrapbooks comes in two sizes: either 8 x 10 inches or 10 x 12 inches. The paper size you choose determines the size of your binder. You can get these supplies at any good craft store.

**Steps for Making a Photo Scrapbook**

1. Decide on a theme for the book. For example, it could be "The Family Vacation to the Beach" or "Our Trip to the Rocky Mountains."

2. Pick out the pictures you want to use and then organize them by different parts of the trip. For example, you might have a page on your day at the beach, or you might have a page about the snowball fight your family had in August in the Rocky Mountains.

   You should plan to put three or four pictures on each page. You can also use several pages for one part of the vacation. Remember, your scrapbook will be done one page at a time.

3. Decide how you want to arrange the pictures on a page. Then put the pictures for each page into separate piles.

4. Choose a color from your paper selection to be the background for one page of photos.

5. Choose a contrasting or coordinating color to mat your pictures. The mat is the border that goes around each picture. Some people do not like to mat their pictures; they prefer to paste their pictures right on the page.

6. Cut the pictures to trim off those parts of the picture you don't like or

need. This is called "cropping" the picture. Cropping gives you more room on your scrapbook page.

7. (If you are not matting your pictures, skip this step.) Put glue on the pictures and attach them to your mat color. Crop the matted pictures, allowing 1 to 2 inches of paper around each one.

8. Lay out your pictures on the background color. You need to leave enough room for a title for the page and captions for each picture. Captions are usually two or three sentences under each picture that explain who is in the picture and what is happening. Don't forget to add the date when the picture was taken.

9. Paste all the pictures on your background paper in the binder. Use your acid-free pen to write the picture captions and page headings.

When you finish the page, you are ready to start the next one. Follow steps 3 through 9 for each page.

Your scrapbook is almost complete when all the pictures you selected in step 2 are pasted to the pages. Before you can call it finished, you must think about what you want to title your scrapbook. Put a title on the cover by using large, handwritten letters or pre-purchased sticker letters. You may even want to design and print out a title using your computer.

**Congratulations –
your photo scrapbook is complete!**

**1. The passage indicates that people make scrapbooks for what reason?**

   A. to sell copies of vacation pictures

   B. to stay busy during the cold winter

   C. to avoid keeping pictures in boxes

   D. to remember trips or special events

*HINT: This question asks you to think about information from the passage. If you are unsure of the answer, skim the passage and think about why someone would like to make scrapbooks.*

**2. How is this passage organized?**

   A. The author tells about how he once made a scrapbook after a favorite vacation.

   B. The author writes about scrapbooks before he gives instructions on how to make one.

   C. The author divides the passages into what to do and what not to do for a task.

   D. The author reviews scrapbooks that he saw while visiting his friends and family.

*HINT: This question asks you to think about the way the author has organized the text. Look at the passage. How are thoughts or ideas separated?*

**3. Why did the author write this passage?**

   A. to describe how to make a scrapbook

   B. to show that making scrapbooks is hard

   C. to tell about his vacation to the beach

   D. to persuade the reader to make scrapbooks

*HINT: This question asks you to draw a conclusion based on the passage. What do you think the author was trying to say in this passage?*

**4. This would be a good passage to read before**

   A. visiting the Rocky Mountains.

   B. throwing away old photographs.

   C. making a scrapbook of a trip.

   D. spending time with your family.

*HINT: This question asks you to think about the passage. How and when would it benefit someone to read this passage?*

**5. What step is optional when making a scrapbook?**

   A. deciding how to arrange pictures

   B. gluing the pictures to the pages

   C. matting the pictures on paper

   D. selecting the pictures to use

*HINT: This question asks you to recall a detail from the passage. If you are unsure of the answer, reread the steps for making the scrapbook.*

**6. What does the author mean when he says that you will need "assorted" colored sheets of paper in paragraph 5?**

   A. a variety of

   B. organized

   C. plain types of

   D. very small

*HINT: This question asks you to clarify some words from the passage. Reread paragraph 4. Are there any clues to the words' meaning in the paragraph?*

**7. What step in making a scrapbook do you do after you have selected a theme and the pictures?**

   A. Crop pictures by trimming off parts.

   B. Decide how to arrange the pictures.

   C. Choose a color from the paper selection.

   D. Lay out the pictures on the background.

*HINT: This question asks you to recall a detail from the passage. If you are unsure of the answer, reread the steps for making a scrapbook.*

**8. What is done after each page is completed?**

   A. It is stacked together in one pile.

   B. It is mailed to a hotel you stayed in.

   C. It is covered in plastic.

   D. It is inserted into a binder.

*HINT: This question asks you to recall a detail from the passage. If you are unsure of the answer, reread the steps for making a scrapbook.*

**FOR THE OPEN-ENDED QUESTION BELOW, REMEMBER TO:**
- Pay attention to what the question is asking you.
- Be sure to answer everything the question asks you.
- Fully explain what you mean by your answer.
- Use details from the story/passage.

9. The author of this passage mentions that scrapbooking is a good activity for families to do together.
   - **Explain how a family might be affected by making a scrapbook together.**

   **Use information from the passage to support your response.**

_____

_____

_____

_____

_____

_____

_____

_____

_____

_____

_____

_____

**FOR THE OPEN-ENDED QUESTION BELOW, REMEMBER TO:**
- Pay attention to what the question is asking you.
- Be sure to answer everything the question asks you.
- Fully explain what you mean by your answer.
- Use details from the story/passage.

10. This passage is organized in a unique way, using both bullet points and numbered steps.
    - **Explain why the author most likely chose to use these types of organizational tools to write this type of passage.**

    **Use information from the passage to support your response.**

# CHAPTER 5

# Going Beyond the Text
## Forming Opinions, Making Judgments, and Drawing Conclusions

**RI.5.10: FORMING OPINIONS**
**RL.5.20: MAKING JUDGMENTS/DRAWING CONCLUSIONS**

To answer some open-ended questions on the test, you may be asked to **form opinions** about what you have read. This chapter will teach you how to form an opinion, first by gathering facts from the text, and then by analyzing how the author used the facts. One of the first things you need to be able to do is to identify whether the author's main purpose was to inform, to entertain, or to persuade.

Similarly, in some questions, you may be asked to **make a judgment** or **draw a conclusion**. While these two tasks may at first sound like they would be the same, there are differences in the way you would approach each. Nonetheless, whether you are making a judgment or drawing a conclusion, you have to know what the author is telling you in the text.

## YOU TRY IT

You have just finished reading a story. Your teacher asks you to write your opinion of the actions of one of the characters in the story. What do you do?

- Do you describe the character's appearance and personality and tell facts about him or her?
- Do you tell all the things the character did in the story?
- Do you write down your feelings about the character?

Your best bet would be to do the last option. You should write about what you thought about who the character was and what the character did.

## RI.5.10: FORMING OPINIONS

### What is an opinion?

How often have you heard or asked this question: "What do you think?" The response would be an opinion.

An **opinion** is what a person thinks. Opinions can't be proven.

A **fact** is based on real information and can be proved to be true.

When you read and when you listen to people, it is important for you to be able to tell the difference between a fact and an opinion.

### What are some examples of facts or opinions?

**Here are some facts. They are based on real information and can be proven.**
• Venus is the only planet in our solar system that rotates clockwise.
• The fingerprints of koala bears are similar in pattern, shape, and size to the fingerprints of humans.
• A quarter has 119 grooves around its edge.
• The first zoo in the United States opened in Philadelphia, Pennsylvania.

**Here are everyday opinions from students.**
• Yesterday's game could not have been more exciting.
• Mom's apple pie is my favorite!
• Science is the most interesting subject in school.
• The speech the principle gave yesterday was inspiring.

**Explore CCSS/PARCC Grade 5 Reading**

## How can I tell what is a fact?

A **fact** can be proven to be true.

If you want to verify a fact, places to look include encyclopedias, dictionaries, an almanac, an atlas, and textbooks.

You could also ask a person who has the knowledge and experience to answer your question.

## How can I tell what is an opinion?

An **opinion** cannot be right or wrong.

There are simply differences of opinion. Whether or not you should take an opinion seriously depends on the honesty, integrity, and knowledge of the person who is speaking or the author who is writing.

**Here is something to watch out for:**
If you take an opinion as fact, it will become real for you. Suppose someone tells you either of these things—"You're a math whiz!" or "You just can't do math!" Both of these statements are one person's opinions.

If you take the person seriously and believe the words, you will either be encouraged or discouraged. Your ability to do your best in math class may be affected. Mixing up facts and opinions can create problems.

**To find out whether something could be a fact, ask yourself— could I find out if this is true?**
If the answer is "yes", then the statement is a **fact**.
If the answer is "no", then the statement is an **opinion.**

## When would I be asked for my opinion on the test?

You may be asked to form an opinion about a story or an article you've read. Then you may be asked to back up your answer with facts and information from the text.

**Here is an example of this kind of question:**
You read about a "Park Clean-Up Day" in a neighboring town. Your teacher has asked you whether or not you think that your town or city—which also has a public park—should hold such an event.

Use details from the passage as well as your own knowledge to form an opinion about whether or not a one-day community effort to clean up the park area would be a good idea for your town or city.

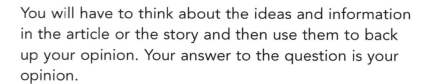

## How would I answer this question?

You will have to think about the ideas and information in the article or the story and then use them to back up your opinion. Your answer to the question is your opinion.

As you write your response, remember to connect your opinion to the story or article you have just read!

That will make your argument or opinion much stronger.

## LET'S TRY IT TOGETHER

**DIRECTIONS**   Read the story/passage and together we will discuss the questions.

# Editorial in the School Newspaper

Leah had signed up to work on the school newspaper in September. So far, she had learned something new at every newspaper staff meeting. Now she is working on an editorial about the school board's latest proposal. The idea is that school would be open year-round except for some short vacations.

Leah herself believes that year-round school is a great idea. She has many reasons to support her point of view. She thinks that, without the long summer break, students would become smarter. Less time would have to be taken reviewing material already covered, and more time could be given to new topics and new learning. Year-round school would be easier on working parents. They would not have to arrange care for young children over the summer break.  Students would have a healthier lifestyle since they would no longer be bored and lazy for several months at a time.

Another point Leah plans to make is that family vacations could be spread out over the year. She thinks that many of the attractions and places that families visit would be less crowded. The reason for the summer break no longer exists, too, since not many people are living on family farms where extra help is needed during the growing season. The time for year-round school, she feels, has come. ■

## How does Leah support her opinion?

Leah uses facts to support her opinion.

**Here are facts Leah used to support her opinion:**
- Students would not be out of school for the lengthy summer vacation, and so they would be able to learn and remember much more.
- Working parents would not need to arrange care for young children during the long summer breaks.

## RL.5.10: MAKING JUDGMENTS/DRAWING CONCLUSIONS

### What does it mean to make a judgment?

Every day, every one of us makes judgments.

When you **make a judgment** about something you've read in a passage, you use what you already know together with information from the passage itself to make a decision.

Making a judgment can be effective in understanding what you are reading.

You have learned that sometimes an author does not come right out and say what he or she really means.

When that happens, the author is relying on the reader to make his or her own judgment about the author's meaning.

**Here are questions to ask yourself when trying to make a judgment based on a passage:**
• What is important? Why?
• How does the author lead the reader from one event to another?
• How does each event in the story affect the rest of the story?
• What is the most likely explanation for the question at hand?

Authors tell readers much more than they come right out and say. They give you hints or clues to help you "read between the lines."

## LET'S TRY IT TOGETHER

| **DIRECTIONS** | Read the passage below and answer the questions that follow. |
| --- | --- |

# Moving to a New Home

Each year, many families move to new homes. They can move across the city, the state, or the country. Moving to a new home can be exciting. However, it can also pose new challenges. How can a fifth grader stay safe and happy after moving to a new home?

Here are some suggestions: Learn your new address and phone number as soon as possible. With your parents, make a visit to your new school before your first day and learn its location. If you will take a bus to school, visit the bus stop and learn the bus number. Plan with your parents what you will do in an emergency and know the people you can contact if you are unable to reach your parents. Take a walking tour of your new neighborhood with your parents. Find out the names of the streets, main roads, landmarks in the area, and any locations you can visit. Enjoy all that is new and look forward to making new friends ■

1. **When you move to a new home, which of the following will be most important for keeping safe?**
   A. taking a tour bus
   B. arranging your new bedroom
   C. having an emergency plan
   D. knowing where the grocery store is

### Could I use my own experience to help?

- Has your family ever moved?
- From your own experience, what was the most important thing you did after you arrived at your new home?

Look at all the above choices and think about which one best answers the question.

## Which answer is the best?

### Is it answer choice A?
Does the paragraph mention a tour bus?

What kind of bus does it mention? Why is the bus mentioned important?

### What about answer choice B?
Did you worry about safety when you arranged the bedroom in your new home?

While there are certainly safety issues to keep in mind inside the house, do you think that this choice correctly answers the question?

### Could it be answer choice C?
Did you and your parents come up with a plan about what to do in an emergency?

Do you think that having this plan would help to keep you safe?

### How about answer choice D?
Would knowing where the grocery store is be important for your personal safety?

Would it be the most important among the choices?

The most important thing for anyone is personal safety. The question asks you to judge which choice is the most important.

Of the choices, an emergency plan is most important since it will enable you to get help when you need it, so **C** is the correct answer.

---

## What does it mean to draw a conclusion?

When you **draw a conclusion**, you pull out the meaning of what you have read.

The word **draw** here does not mean sketching or making a picture; it means to "pull out." (e.g., If you draw on your imagination, you will surely write a creative story.)

You put together all the information in what you have read so that you can pull out a meaning or idea. In order to draw a conclusion that makes sense, you must show strong evidence from the story or article.

## How do I draw a conclusion?

**To draw a conclusion, you want to follow several steps.**

- Start by identifying the main idea and the supporting details.
- Think about what you already know about the topic.
- Then put the information from the story or article together with what you already know to draw a conclusion.

Once you have reached your conclusion, either think about what you have read or review the passage.

You will want to make sure that the conclusion you have reached seems correct.

## LET'S TRY IT TOGETHER

**DIRECTIONS**   Read the passage below and answer the question that follow.

# Special Birthday

Ruth and Marika had been writing to each other ever since they were very small. Because Ruth's mother was Marika's father's sister, the two girls were cousins.

However, because the families lived in different countries, the girls had never seen each other. When their correspondence began, the letters had been very short and illustrated with the girls' drawings.

Now as they were growing older, they found more to write about, so their letters were longer and filled with news of school, sports, and other activities.

Even though Tuesday would be Ruth's eleventh birthday and there would be a family gathering in the evening to celebrate, she wasn't expecting much. However, when she came home from school that day, her mother was scurrying about.

"Dinner will be a little later this evening, since Dad got delayed," she told Ruth, "so please get dressed up for this special day." After Ruth had changed her clothes, her mother had everything ready. The sound of excited voices told them that Dad had arrived, and he was not alone. Four people walked into the house with him, all wearing big smiles. The parents stood back with the older boy as a smiling girl about Ruth's age came over to greet her. ▪

**1. Who had come to help celebrate Ruth's birthday?**
   A. the family who lived next door
   B. the twins from her class at school and their parents
   C. business friends of her father's
   D. Marika, her brother, and their parents

## How would I answer this question?

First, you should look for information within the text.

**What clues do we get from the text?**
• Ruth is not expecting much activity for her birthday.
• Her parents seem to be very busy.
• Ruth's father comes home from work with four people.
• Ruth's father and the group of people seem to know each other well.

## Which answer is best?

Then, think about your own experiences.

**What experiences could you draw from?**
• Have you ever been surprised for your birthday?
• How were people behaving?
• Did you ever help plan a surprise for someone? What made you decide what to plan?

**Finally, take a look at the choices mentioned in the answer options.**

**A  the family who lived next door**

Could this be the answer?  Was there anything in the passage about the people who lived next door? Think about the facts that we do know. This is probably not the correct answer.

**B  the twins from her class at school and their parents**

This probably is not the correct answer. There was nothing in the passage about Ruth's classmates.

**C  business friends of her father's**

Could this be the answer? We do learn in the passage that Ruth's father had been delayed, and perhaps he was coming home from work. However, that does not give you enough information to choose this answer. Also, it seems it would be somewhat strange for a father to bring guests from work home for dinner on his daughter's birthday.

**D  Marika, her brother, and their parents**

This may very well be the correct answer. The relationship between Ruth and her cousin Marika is important to the information in the passage. The parents of each girl probably would have been happy if the two could meet. It would be a wonderful surprise for Ruth's birthday. However, you do have to remember that it is important to look at all the answer options.

Putting together all the information from the passage with your own experience, you should draw the conclusion that Marika and her family have traveled a long way to come and visit for Ruth's birthday. Ruth's father was probably delayed because he had picked them up from the airport.

Answer choice **D** is correct.

## YOU TRY IT

| **DIRECTIONS INTRODUCTION** | Read this story/passage and answer the questions that follow. This passage tells about a new type of honeybee that is found in parts of North and South America. Read the passage and learn about Africanized "killer" bees. |
| --- | --- |

# Africanized "Killer" Bees

**The Development of Killer Bees**
A new strain of bee has appeared in warm climates. These bees will attack anything that comes near their hives. These Africanized honeybees are the same species and are nearly identical to the European honeybees, which we're most familiar with in this country.

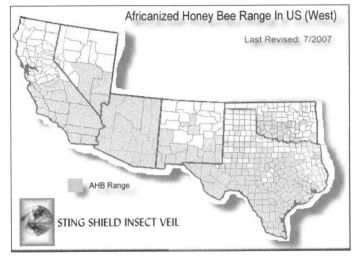

*Figure 1*

In 1957, African honeybees were brought to Brazil. Scientists were trying to breed a better honeybee, one that would make more honey. However, soon after the African bees arrived, an accident occurred in the labs. Many of the new bees escaped.

**CHECK FOR UNDERSTANDING**

Why do you think that these "killer bees" are found in warmer climates?

Soon, people began reporting that some honeybees were acting more aggressively. They swarmed after things in large numbers. While these bees looked like honeybees, they attacked people more often. In a short time, the hives of these "new" bees were found all over Brazil.

People started calling these bees "killer bees" because of the way they attacked. Typical European honeybees stay around their nest to protect it. This new strain of bee seemed to explode from the nest when disturbed. They would defend their nest by swarming around the intruder. These bees would even follow a person for a distance of up to a quarter of a mile. During the time they swarmed, the killer bees would repeatedly sting a person. One person was stung over 500 times before the bees were driven away. Some people have even died from being stung by killer bees.

The venom of a killer bee is no stronger than that of a normal honeybee. After they sting, both the female killer bees and the European honeybees lose their stingers. The reason a person is usually hurt by killer bees is that their swarms contain many more bees. Thus, a person might be stung many times. The increased amount of venom from so many stings is very dangerous.

Killer bees are also a problem to beekeepers and to agriculture. Honeybees are used to pollinate plants each year. Without pollination, many of the foods we eat would not grow. When killer bees mix with the normal honeybee queens, the new bees are more aggressive. Beekeepers cannot use these new bees to pollinate crops. They will swarm and sting anything that moves. As the killer bee population grows in an area, it causes major problems for agriculture. To keep producing their crops, farmers are forced to find other honeybees.

**Spread of the Killer Bees**
Since 1957, Africanized bees have been spreading about 200 miles a year. They are found as far south as Argentina. Today, these bees may be found in Alabama, Arkansas, Florida, Louisiana, California, Nevada, Arizona, New Mexico, Texas, and Oklahoma. The maps in *Figure 1* and *Figure 2* shows the states in which killer bees have been found as of July 2007.

**8** The spread of killer bees has slowed in recent years. Some scientists feel that the cooler weather is the reason for this lack of movement. Others feel this is just a lull. They expect the expansion to pick up in future years. No one knows for sure what will happen.

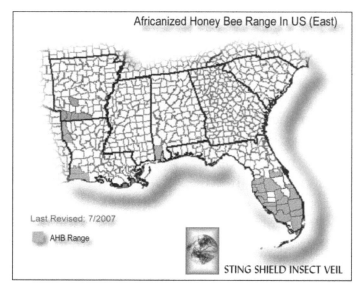

Figure 2

**Methods of Control**
Two methods of controlling the Africanized bees have been tried. Both try to reduce the aggressive strain of the killer bees. One is called "drone flooding." This involves putting large numbers of new European honeybees

into an area. It is hoped that this will result in the killer bee queen mating with the less aggressive honeybees. Then the resulting honeybees would be more like European honeybees.

The second method is called "re-queening." In this method, beekeepers replace their queens each year. This helps assure that the resulting drone honeybees are not aggressive.

At this point, no one knows if either method will work. However, it is important that something be tried. Wherever killer bees have appeared, problems arise. If they are not controlled, the problems will only get worse.

Homeowners should never attempt to control any bee hive. If you live in an area where Africanized bee colonies have been seen, you should contact a local expert to have any threatening hives removed. A local beekeeper will likely be happy to safely remove the hive. ∎

**1. What does the word "lull" mean in paragraph 8?**

A. break

B. game

C. mess

D. accident

*HINT: This question asks you to identify the meaning of the word "lull." If you are unsure of the answer, reread paragraph 8. Are there any clues to the word's meaning in the sentence the word is used in?*

**2. Why are Africanized honeybees more dangerous than European honeybees?**

A. Their venom is stronger.

B. Their hives are larger.

C. Their stingers are sharper.

D. Their attacks are more aggressive.

*HINT: This question asks you to recall a detail from the passage. If you are unsure of the answer, reread the fourth paragraph.*

**3. Why did the author most likely write this passage?**

A. to teach readers how to avoid killer bees

B. to inform readers about killer bees

C. to entertain readers with stories about killer bees

D. to tell readers how to stop the spread of killer bees

*HINT: This question asks you to make a judgment based on what you have read in the passage. What do you think the author's purpose was when he wrote this?*

**4. When beekeepers "re-queen," they**

A. put large numbers of queens in one area.

B. replace their queen bees each year.

C. use the same queens over and over.

D. relocate their queens a few times a year.

*HINT: This question asks you to recall a detail from the passage. If you are unsure of the answer, reread the "Methods of Control" section of the passage.*

**5. How many times can female killer bees sting?**

A. one time
B. two times
C. five times
D. ten times

*HINT: This question asks you to recall a detail from the passage. If you are unsure of the answer, reread the fifth paragraph.*

**6. What do some scientists believe is the reason the spread of killer bees has slowed in recent years?**

A. re-queening
B. drone flooding
C. cooler weather
D. warmer weather

*HINT: This question asks you to draw a conclusion based on the passage. If you are unsure of the answer, reread the "Spread of Killer Bees" section.*

**7. What does the word "strain" mean in the phrase "a new strain of bee"?**

A. type
B. twist
C. injury
D. struggle

*HINT: This question asks you to clarify some words from the passage. Reread the first paragraph, looking for clues to the word's meaning.*

**8. Read the following sentence from the passage.**

"Homeowners should *never* attempt to control any bee hive."

**The author put the word *"never"* in italics to**

A. improve how the paragraph sounds.
B. highlight a specific detail in the paragraph.
C. break up the paragraph into sections.
D. emphasize the idea in the paragraph.

*HINT: This question asks you to think about the way the author uses words. Did the italics change the way you thought about the sentence? How?*

**FOR THE OPEN-ENDED QUESTION BELOW, REMEMBER TO:**
- Pay attention to what the question is asking you.
- Be sure to answer everything the question asks you.
- Fully explain what you mean by your answer.
- Use details from the story/passage.

9. The reason for the spread of Africanized "killer" bees from Brazil was because of an accident in a scientific laboratory.
   - Predict what might have happened if that accident had not occurred and the scientists had carried out their experiment as planned.
   - Consider the nature of the killer bee species in your answer.

   Use information from the passage to support your response.

**FOR THE OPEN-ENDED QUESTION BELOW, REMEMBER TO:**
• Pay attention to what the question is asking you.
• Be sure to answer everything the question asks you.
• Fully explain what you mean by your answer.
• Use details from the story/passage.

10. In the passage, the author states, "If they are not controlled, the problems will only get worse."

   • **Explain what the author means by this statement.**

   • **Refer to Figure 1 and Figure 2 in your explanation.**

   **Use information from the passage to support your response.**

_____

_____

_____

_____

_____

_____

_____

_____

_____

_____

_____

_____

_____

_____

_____

_____

_____

_____

## YOU TRY IT

| | |
|---|---|
| **DIRECTIONS**<br>**INTRODUCTION** | Read this passage and answer the questions that follow. The following safety tips have been put into this pamphlet in order to protect a person from getting stung by honeybees. |

# Safety Tips to Avoid Getting Stung by Bees

Everyone wants to avoid getting stung by honeybees. These guidelines will help you avoid serious injury from honeybee stings. This information can be applied to killer bees as well.

 You should watch for bees that come in and out of any opening when you enter a new area.

**Look carefully at such things as:**

- cracks in a wall
- holes in discarded boxes
- holes in the ground
- dead trees
- any place where a honeybee could hide
- Notice if there are a number of bees near the same or adjacent openings. If there are, move quickly away from that area.
- Listen for the hum of an active bee colony as you walk around an area. The buzzing will sound like a lot of bees are together in one spot. If you hear that type of hum, move away from the area quickly. There is probably a hive nearby. Of course, if you see only a few bees in nearby flowers, this is not a reason to flee. Bees moving among flowers is normal.
- Be alert for bees that are acting strangely. Often, you will have some warning that bees are beginning to defend their hives. If you see a number of them flying around a certain area, leave. Also, if you see what you think are other types of unusual behavior for bees, vacate the area quickly.
- Be careful when moving stones or wood that has been lying around for a while. There may be a nest of bees under whatever you are moving.
- When you are in a wilderness area, keep an eye out for bees just as you would for other animals like snakes.

If bees do begin to circle your body, quickly look for a way to escape. If possible, cover your head and upper body and run away as fast as you can. If you can't find anything to throw over your head, at least pull a shirt or sweater over your face. This will offer limited protection as you exit the area.

Find shelter, such as in a building or a car, that allows you to shut out the bees. Hopefully, the bees will not follow you into the shelter you have chosen. If they do, keep moving until you have lost most of the bees.

Do not jump into water to escape the bees. Bees, especially killer bees, will usually swarm around the place where you entered the water. When you come up for air, they will start stinging you again.

As soon as you are in a safe place, check your body to see if you have been stung. If you have been stung multiple times and there is severe swelling, seek medical attention. If you are allergic to bee stings, immediately see a doctor.

Do not squeeze stingers in your body with fingers or tweezers. The venom sac is usually still attached to the stinger in your skin. If you squeeze the stinger, more venom will be injected into your body. If you must remove the stingers, use a piece of flat cardboard or a credit card to push the stingers out. ∎

**14**

✔ **CHECK FOR UNDERSTANDING**

Why do you think bees would be found in the places listed?

---

**1. Why did the author most likely write this passage?**

    A. to entertain readers with facts about honeybees

    B. to teach readers how to treat honeybee stings

    C. to describe the places in which honeybees live

    D. to tell readers how to avoid injuries from honeybees

*HINT: This question asks you to make a judgment based on what you have read in the passage. What do you think the author's purpose was?*

**2. What does the word "injected" mean in paragraph 14?**

    A. removed

    B. pushed

    C. discovered

    D. attached

*HINT: This question asks you to identify the meaning of the word "injected." If you are unsure of the answer, reread paragraph 14. Are there any clues to the word's meaning in the sentence the word is used in?*

**3. The purpose of paragraph 14 is to**

    A. tell what stingers can do if left in your skin.

    B. give a summary of the guidelines explained in the passage.

    C. explain what to do if stingers are left in your body.

    D. teach you how to avoid getting stung by bees.

*HINT: This question also asks you to think about why the author wrote the fourteenth paragraph. Reread paragraph 14. What does the paragraph tell you?*

**4. What should you do if bees begin to circle your body?**

    A. throw a piece of stone or wood

    B. jump into water and try to stay under

    C. keep your arms still at your sides

    D. cover your head and upper body

*HINT: This question asks you to recall a detail. If you are unsure of the answer, reread the last column of the pamphlet.*

**5. Which is a good place to hide when running from bees?**

    A. in a pool

    B. in a tree

    C. in a house

    D. in a garden

*HINT: This question asks you to draw a conclusion based on the passage. If you are unsure of the answer, reread the last column of the pamphlet.*

**6. Which sentence tells what this passage is mostly about?**

    A. There are guidelines to help you avoid serious injury should you spot bees in the woods.

    B. If you have been stung by bees and there is severe swelling, you should seek medical attention.

    C. If you remove bee stingers, you can use flat cardboard or a credit card.

    D. If you see a few bees circling some flowers, you should leave the area.

*HINT: This question asks you to identify the central idea of the passage. Think about what you have read. What did this passage make you think about?*

**7. The author most likely chose to use bullet points in this passage to**

    A. improve how the passage sounds.

    B. highlight a specific detail in the passage.

    C. break up the passage into sections.

    D. emphasize the idea in the passage.

*HINT: This question asks you to think about the way the author has organized the text. Did the bullet points change the way you thought about the passage? How?*

**FOR THE OPEN-ENDED QUESTION BELOW, REMEMBER TO:**
• Pay attention to what the question is asking you.
• Be sure to answer everything the question asks you.
• Fully explain what you mean by your answer.
• Use details from the story/passage.

8. The author lists several places where honeybees like to build their hives.
   • Explain why honeybees most likely choose these types of locations for their hives.
   Use information from the passage to support your response.

**FOR THE OPEN-ENDED QUESTION BELOW, REMEMBER TO:**
- Pay attention to what the question is asking you.
- Be sure to answer everything the question asks you.
- Fully explain what you mean by your answer.
- Use details from the story/passage.

9. You read in your local newspaper a story about a man who was chased through the woods, into a pond, and then to his home by honeybees. You decide to interview him for the school newspaper to help students understand how to prevent this sort of thing from happening to them.
   - **Come up with three questions you would ask this man.**
   - **Using what you know about the best way to avoid being chased by honeybees, explain how the man could have avoided being chased over such a long distance.**

   Use information from the passage to support your response.

## YOU TRY IT

| DIRECTIONS INTRODUCTION | Read this passage and answer the questions that follow. Costa Rica is a country with a wide range of climates, from dry plateaus to rich tropical forests. Naturalists find it a wonderful place to study a variety of plants and animals. Some are found no place else in the world. This passage tells a little about this area of Central America. |
|---|---|

# One Country's Treasures

Costa Rica is a small Central American country. It is perhaps the most peaceful country in the world. It is also a wonder of nature because of its diverse climates. Costa Rica is sandwiched between two oceans, the Pacific Ocean on its west coast and the Atlantic Ocean on its east coast. A high mountain ridge runs down the middle of the country. It also has a number of active volcanoes. The land's location and shape result in 12 tropical life zones.

Each zone has a large number of different plants and animals. Costa Rica takes pains to try to preserve all of its natural resources. There are many that need protection. How huge is this task? Let's look at just the number of animal species identified by naturalists. Costa Rica has 850 kinds of birds and 200 kinds of mammals. Insects top more than 35,000 species. More than 200 types of reptiles and about 150 types of amphibians also live there.

**2**

Have you ever wished you could touch a cloud? Well, in Monteverde you actually walk through low clouds. Monteverde is a very wet, mountainous area. Approximately 150 inches of rain accumulate each year to create lush plant growth. It is home to huge numbers and types of animals. Several groups of people are responsible for having preserved this land.

### ✔ CHECK FOR UNDERSTANDING

Why would it be important to know about the plants and animals of Costa Rica?

Prior to the Korean War, which began in 1950, forty-four Quakers moved from the

United States to Monteverde, mainly because they were peace-loving and Costa Rica had no army. The Quakers settled on about 3,700 acres. Part of it they farmed. The other part they set aside as a preserve. It was their way of saving some of the land and its animals.

With help from the World Wildlife Fund, local groups were able to buy many acres of land. They created, in 1972, the Monteverde Cloud Forest Preserve, which brought about important social, economic, and environmental changes to the communities in the area.

With the loss of this land to the conservation group,[1] local farmers and loggers had to find new ways to earn money. One way was for them to become nature guides. In order to do this, they needed to be educated. Many visitors to Costa Rica spoke English, so the guides were taught English.

Besides buying land, funds were used for other purposes. One was to teach about the forest and its animals. Programs began for children, teachers, and community groups. Trips for schoolchildren started as well. Few had ever been to the rain forest and many had seen neither the animals nor their habitat. These programs continue today.

One part of this reserve in Monteverde is extra-special. In 1988, far away in Sweden, a young boy learned about the reserve in school. He wanted to help save more land for the animals. His class decided to raise funds to help buy more land. Their money bought 15 acres of forestland in Monteverde. It became known as the Children's Eternal Forest. Children from 44 countries—through fund raising—helped buy more land through this fund. This forest has now grown to 42,500 acres. Their funds keep helping. Now the money is also used to save other forests in other places.

Today, Quakers still form a large part of the overall population alongside the native Costa Ricans. There are currently three main Quaker families: the Guindons, the Rockwells, and the Beeche-Campbells. The town of Monteverde is now trying to survive solely by offering outdoor eco-friendly tourist activities, such as hiking, mountain biking, and horseback riding. ■

[1]**conservation group:** *an association of people organized to work for the benefit of some part of the environment*

1. **Which of these statements is an opinion about Costa Rica?**
   A. It is a small Central American country.
   B. It has two oceans on its borders.
   C. It is the most peaceful country in the world.
   D. It has a tall mountain range in the middle.

   *HINT: This question asks you identify an opinion. Read your answer options. Which of the answer cannot be proven with facts?*

2. **This passage would be *best* to read if you were working on a report about**
   A. very small countries.
   B. protecting the wildlife.
   C. becoming a tour guide.
   D. starting a fundraiser.

   *HINT: This question asks you to think about what you have read in the passage. From your answer options, the information in the passage would be most helpful for which topic?*

3. **Why do all the groups work to save the rain forest in Costa Rica?**
   A. because the country does not have an army
   B. because the loggers and farmers lost jobs
   C. because the two oceans are good places to fish and surf
   D. because many animals and plants live in a small space

   *HINT: This question asks you to make a judgment based on what you have read in the passage. For what reason do you think the groups work in the rain forest?*

4. **Which of these groups represents the largest variety of animals?**
   A. birds
   B. mammals
   C. reptiles
   D. amphibians

   *HINT: This question asks you to recall a detail. If you are unsure of the answer, reread the second paragraph.*

5. **What job did men and women take when they could not be farmers and loggers?**
   A. naturalists
   B. English teachers
   C. nature guides
   D. Quakers

*HINT: This question asks you to recall a detail from the passage. If you are unsure of the answer, reread the middle of the passage.*

6. **Why would peace-loving Quakers settle in Costa Rica?**
   A. They wanted to live in a mountainous country.
   B. Costa Rica has a lot of rainfall for growing crops.
   C. They liked the idea of living high among the clouds.
   D. Costa Rica is a country that does not have an army.

*HINT: This question asks you to make a judgment based on what you have read in the passage. What would peaceful people like about Costa Rica?*

7. **Which best describes the main idea of this passage?**
   A. There are many things to do on a vacation to Central America.
   B. Many people have helped protect certain areas of Costa Rica.
   C. The only way to protect the environment is to buy forest land.
   D. It is better to go into the mountains than to stay by the ocean.

*HINT: This question asks you to identify the central idea of the passage. Think about what you have read. What did this passage make you think about?*

8. **What does the word "identified" mean as it is used in paragraph 2?**
   A. recognized
   B. searched
   C. eaten
   D. captured

*HINT: This question asks you to identify the meaning of the word "identified." If you are unsure of the answer, reread paragraph 2. Are there any clues to the word's meaning in the sentence the word is used in?*

**9. Where is the Children's Eternal Forest located?**

    A.  in Sweden

    B.  in the United States

    C.  in Monteverde

    D.  in 44 different countries

*HINT: This question asks you to recall a detail from the passage. If you are unsure of the answer, reread the last two paragraphs..*

**10. Why did the author include information about the Children's Eternal Forest in this passage?**

    A.  to persuade readers that children should have a forest named for them

    B.  to show that only children in Sweden care about forests and animals

    C.  to tell how children can organize fundraisers to buy land in their cities

    D.  to describe how children throughout the world can help the Earth

*HINT: This question asks you to make a judgment based on what you have read in the passage. What do you think the author's goal was in including the Children's Eternal Forest?*

**FOR THE OPEN-ENDED QUESTION BELOW, REMEMBER TO:**
• Pay attention to what the question is asking you.
• Be sure to answer everything the question asks you.
• Fully explain what you mean by your answer.
• Use details from the story/passage.

11. **Read this sentence from the passage.**

    "With the loss of this land to the conservation group, local farmers and loggers had to find new ways to earn money."

    • **Explain what had happened to the local farmers and loggers to require them to find new sources for money.**

    **Use information from the passage to support your response.**

**FOR THE OPEN-ENDED QUESTION BELOW, REMEMBER TO:**
- Pay attention to what the question is asking you.
- Be sure to answer everything the question asks you.
- Fully explain what you mean by your answer.
- Use details from the story/passage.

12. The boy from Sweden did a very important and special thing in raising money for preserving forests in Costa Rica.
    - What is something in or near your community that you think should be saved or preserved?
    - Explain how you would go about saving or preserving it.

    Use information from the passage to support your response.

**DIRECTIONS**
**INTRODUCTION**

Read this passage and answer the questions that follow. The following letters appeared in a local newspaper in Arizona over a two-week span. Each talks about what needs to be done to ensure that the Gila monster does not become extinct.

SUNDAY JANUARY 8            **THE PHOENIX GAZETTE**            F5

## EDITORIAL

# Help to Save the Gila Monster

Dear Editor:

The Gila monster is in danger of being lost forever. At one time, Arizona hikers saw Gila monsters regularly. Each year there have been fewer sightings of this lizard. I believe that it is time to do something in order to protect these shy, beautiful animals.

There are a number of things that can be done. Expansion into areas where Gila monsters live must stop. We can't allow farms in Gila habitats.

People should not be allowed to live in these areas. When farms and homes are built in Gila habitats, the Gilas usually die. Protection of their habitat is vital to their survival.

By law, the Gila is a protected species. A person is not even allowed to catch one without a permit. People who collect them for the pet trade can only catch a certain number each year. While **9** helpful, these measures are not enough. The number of Gila monsters continues to shrink. Experts say there may only be about 350 left in the wild.

We need to change the laws protecting these lizards. At present, any Gila monster that comes onto a person's property can be moved.

It's considered a nuisance. Sometimes, rangers will move Gilas less than 200 yards. At other times, Gilas are moved to an entirely new location. However, no one has studied the impact on the Gila of the move to a new area.

We need to know the best way to remove a Gila that is considered to be a nuisance. In this way, it can be moved without being harmed.

Gila monsters are brightly colored. People like to keep them as pets. Allowing Gila monsters to be caught and kept as pets also must stop.

Though there are limits to the number that can be caught for pets, even this small number reduces Gila population. If we allow this to continue, those left in the wild will be reduced even more.

More research needs to be done on the Gila monster. The

Gila is shy. Little is known about the basic aspects of its biology. We have limited information about how Gilas mate and raise their young.

Are there things that could be done to increase the number of babies that grow to adulthood? Without this type of information, no planning for the future can be done.

*(See Save Gila Monsters, continued on page F6)*

*"Experts say there may only be about 350 [Gila Monsters] left in the wild."*

**CHECK FOR UNDERSTANDING**

Why do you think the newspaper editor put these two editorials next to each other?

SUNDAY JANUARY 8     THE PHOENIX GAZETTE     F6

## EDITORIAL

*(Save Gila Monsters, continued from page F5)*

**12** The Gila monster will become extinct in a short time if these steps are not taken now. Yes, some problems will be caused by putting these suggestions into effect. However, there is no other way to ensure that our children will see live Gilas. Let's let our state representatives know it is time to act to save the Gila monster. Write to your state leaders and tell them to "Save the Gila Monster!"

Sincerely,
John Smithers

# We Should Leave Gila Monsters Alone

Dear Editor:

Some people say that unless we take drastic action, the Gila monster is in danger of becoming extinct. They say that there are only 350 of these lizards left in the United States. These people believe that the Gila monster will disappear unless major changes are made. Well, **13** they are wrong! The Gila monster has existed for thousands of years. It will continue to exist in the future, as long as its habitat remains intact.

The people who say there are only 350 Gila monsters left do not explain how they arrived at that number. Is that because few Gilas exist? Or is it because the Gilas were hiding when they did the survey? The Gila monster has excellent vision and hearing. It can sense an animal from far away. This is what makes it such a good predator. Few people see Gilas because the Gilas don't want to be seen.

Last week, I tried an experiment to see if I could find Gila monsters. I waited under a mesquite tree for an hour after dawn. I wanted to see if there were any Gila monsters in the area. About a half-hour later, I saw a Gila stick its head out of a burrow and look around. When I moved, it immediately slipped back into its burrow. I did this in different locations over three days. I saw two Gila monsters. I think the scientists counting the Gilas did not see them because these lizards did not want to be seen.

There are laws protecting the Gila monster in every state it lives in. These laws limit the number of Gilas captured. These laws are sufficient. We don't need to write any new laws. I think we need to ensure that the habitats of the Gila monster remain intact. We should limit future development near these habitats. More homes should not be built in these areas. Existing farms should not be allowed to increase their acreage. That is all that needs to be done to protect this lizard.

If we ensure that the habitat of the Gila monster is preserved, we will ensure the future of the creature. Future generations should and will be able to see this colorful lizard.

Sincerely,
Joanne Miller

1. **The purpose of the first paragraph of "Help to Save the Gila Monster" is to**
   A. share what John Smithers thinks is causing problems for Gila monsters.
   B. explain that Gila monsters are slow, shy lizards.
   C. teach why people do not see as many Gila monsters today.
   D. emphasize that Gila monsters are in danger of becoming extinct.

   HINT: *This question asks why the author wrote the first paragraph. Reread paragraph 1. What does the paragraph tell you?*

2. **What does the word "reduced" mean in paragraph 9?**
   A. grown
   B. lessened
   C. changed
   D. broken

   HINT: *This question asks you to identify the meaning of the word "reduced." If you are unsure of the answer, reread paragraph 9. Are there any clues to the word's meaning in the sentence the word is used in?*

3. **Why does Joanne Miller think few people see Gila monsters?**
   A. because too many people catch Gila monsters to keep as pets
   B. because there are only 350 Gila monsters left
   C. because Gila monsters don't want to be seen
   D. because Gila monsters have moved to new locations

   HINT: *This question asks you to draw a conclusion based on what you have read in the passage. Reread Joanne Miller's editorial and think what she was saying about Gila monsters being seen.*

4. **Why did John Smithers most likely write "Save the Gila Monster"?**
   A. to persuade readers to act to help Gila monsters
   B. to inform readers of the reasons why Gila monsters are protected
   C. to tell readers what Gila monsters look like
   D. to teach readers about the foods that Gila monsters eat

   HINT: *This question asks you to make a judgment based on what you have read in the passage. What do you think John Smithers's purpose was when he wrote his editorial?*

**5. The purpose of the twelfth paragraph is to**
   A. tell readers about plans to develop Gila monsters' habitats in the future.
   B. entertain readers with funny stories about Gila monsters.
   C. inform readers about the steps involved in Joanne Miller's experiment.
   D. persuade readers that Gila monsters' habitats should be protected.

*HINT: This question asks why the author wrote the twelfth paragraph. Reread paragraph 12. What does the paragraph tell you?*

**6. How are the arguments of John Smithers and Joanne Miller alike?**
   A. Both think that new laws need to be written to protect the Gila monster.
   B. Both believe that the habitat of the Gila monster needs to be protected.
   C. Both have completed experiments to see if they could find Gila monsters.
   D. Both agree that more Gila monsters should be captured and kept as pets.

*HINT: This question asks you to make a judgment based on what you have read in the passage. Were there any points that both authors made?*

**7. What does the word "existed" mean in paragraph 13?**
   A. died
   B. wandered
   C. lived
   D. feasted

*HINT: This question asks you to identify the meaning of the word "existed." If you are unsure of the answer, reread paragraph 13. Are there any clues to the word's meaning in the sentence the word is used in?*

**8. How does Joanne Miller suggest limiting future development near Gila monsters' habitats?**
   A. Allow animal collectors to capture Gila monsters without a permit.
   B. Don't allow rangers to move Gila monsters to new locations.
   C. Don't allow existing farms to increase their acreage.
   D. Allow more houses to be built near Gila monsters' habitats.

*HINT: This question asks you to draw a conclusion based on what you have read in the passage. If you are unsure of the answer, reread the beginning of Joanne Miller's editorial.*

**FOR THE OPEN-ENDED QUESTION BELOW, REMEMBER TO:**
• Pay attention to what the question is asking you.
• Be sure to answer everything the question asks you.
• Fully explain what you mean by your answer.
• Use details from the story/passage.

9. Both John Smithers and Joanne Miller have strong feelings about how to protect Gila monsters.
   • Summarize what John Smithers thinks about how to protect Gila monsters.
   • Summarize what Joanne Miller thinks about how to protect Gila monsters.
   • Include four claims that each author makes.

   Use information from the passage to support your answer.

**FOR THE OPEN-ENDED QUESTION BELOW, REMEMBER TO:**
• Pay attention to what the question is asking you.
• Be sure to answer everything the question asks you.
• Fully explain what you mean by your answer.
• Use details from the story/passage.

10. **When you read editorial letters, you often form an opinion of your own based on the claims made by the authors of those letters.**

    • **In this discussion, do you agree more with John Smithers or Joanne Miller?**

    • **Explain why you feel this way.**

    **Use information from the article to support your response.**

_____

_____

_____

_____

_____

_____

_____

_____

_____

_____

_____

CPSIA information can be obtained at www.ICGtesting.com
Printed in the USA
LVOW01s2115270814

401204LV00014B/620/P